ADDICTION PAPERS

Addiction Papers

From the Perspective of Depth Psychology

By John E. Smethers, Ph.D

Addiction Papers: From the Perspective of Depth Psychology

ISBN-13: 978-1-906628-69-7

Published by CheckPoint Press, Ireland

"Books With Something To Say"

www.checkpointpress.com

CheckPoint
Press

Cover design, book design and editing by CheckPoint Press

Registered with the US Library of Congress and the British Library

This book is dedicated to my parents
John and Evelyn Smethers

Written as a student at
Pacifica Graduate Institute in Carpinteria, California.

TABLE OF CONTENTS

INTRODUCTION

A Biographical Sketch

From grammar school through high school, teachers periodically made comments on my grade reports such as, "John is a capable student but he will not apply himself." They were right. I did just enough to get elevated to the next grade. My dad wouldn't let me quit. Because I was 17 during my entire senior year, I needed parental consent. Though I wasn't enthusiastic academically, my father still managed to instill a value for education that would surface in my life almost 30 years later.

My lack of academic initiative was exacerbated by the ethos of the 1950s. Rock and Roll and James Dean was spurning out a breed of rebels without a cause that turned into the hippies and druggies of the 1960s. So it was with me. In 1956 when I was eleven years old, upon entering junior high school, I started drinking on weekends. Unlike youngsters of later generations, I didn't start experimenting with drugs until the summer of my high school graduation in 1962. I certainly would have if it had been offered to me. In a nutshell, I went to a party when I was eleven and didn't get back until I was 45. Over a period of more than 30 years, there was scarcely a time when I wasn't doing time, paying fines or restitution, doing community service, serving probation or parole, pending court, or suffering the loss of my driver license. I thought of those repercussions as *dues* that I had to pay to continue to live the way I wanted to.

My parents were awesome. Being their only child, I pretty much got whatever I wanted and did whatever I wanted to do - they were not strict disciplinarians, though I did spend my share of time on parental restriction. Nor was I abused in any way; therefore, I don't blame them for my drug and alcohol use. I got high to have fun. Having fun was my goal in life and I avoided responsibility like it was a germ.

By the end of my 15th summer in 1960, I was an alcoholic. Three times within a six- month period, I landed in jail. Each time I'd been drinking.

My first night in jail was for Curfew. Probably the most significant thing about my first arrest was meeting a new friend who remains one of my best friends today. Jim and I had one hell of a good time in that jail cell, climbing around on the bars like monkeys, tearing up the mattresses for cotton ball fights, and yelling obscenities at the cops.

From that point on, going to jail wasn't much of a threat. A week later another friend and I were busted for petty theft - stealing milk off of someone's porch because our mouths were dry from drinking Ripple wine all night. Eight months later, I was arrested for my first DUI on my Cushman Eagle motor scooter. My coveted driver license was revoked before I got it. I was jailed again the night after graduation in 1962 for trespassing and again later that year for stealing hubcaps. There were five arrests and convictions in 1963 for minor offenses (alcohol related), two of which got me 60 days in the county jail.

Once incarcerated at Glen Helen Rehabilitation Center near San Bernardino, two of my friends joined me there. We played practical jokes on each other, met new drug connections, and planned what we were going to do when we got out. It was not an unpleasant experience. Not only was being jailed for the night not much of a threat, serving time wasn't either. After I was released, one of my friends asked, "Well, how did you like it?"

I smiled and said, "I liked it." Compared to what I was expecting, I did like it. To me, it was like being in a summer boy's camp.

I was a happy kid, a happy-go-lucky teenager, and later a relatively happy drug addict. So why did I quit? Because my life was going nowhere, my family was concerned about me, and I knew my mind and body wouldn't take the abuse much longer, so after more than 30 years of drug and alcohol addiction, I quit. It was a process, however, rather than a simple decision. Would I change anything if I had it to do over again?

No!

Why not?

Because I wouldn't be who I am today if my life had been lived differently. In my opinion, *happiness* is part of a temperament that is innate. Of course, life circumstances can alter that, but I believe that the basic temperament is static. If trauma doesn't strike, and we have had a stable and loving foundation in early childhood, most of us are capable of handling most of life's encumbrances. That's my opinion, anyway. However, I don't believe I could have remained very happy had I not stopped drinking and using drugs. Trauma - physical, mental, or spiritual would have inevitably struck.

Before I elaborate any more on my shadow side, I should comment on the shining star of my life - my daughter Lynda. We lost her mother when she was four years old, so before and after and between wives and girlfriends, I raised her. She sends me a mother's day card every year. She and I agree that my drug and alcohol addiction during her childhood has not damaged her. She inevitably became an addict herself, however, but she found recovery after only five years of drug and alcohol abuse. She got clean and sober before I did, and then she hoped and prayed that I would also find recovery. Today, Lynda and I are best friends, and she has brought two more shining stars into my life.

Fortunately, my two grand kids will never have to see me the way my daughter did. They'll never have to watch the police take me out of the house in handcuffs like my daughter did. They'll never have to control their behavior according to what drug I'm taking like my daughter did. And they'll never have to endure being embarrassed in public like my daughter did. The most important thing I can share today, is that it hasn't been necessary for me to take a drink or put a needle in my arm since 7 May 1990 (my last relapse date), and for that I am eternally grateful.

I have been arrested more than 40 times for various misdemeanor and felony offenses, served five county jail sentences, many probations, and a three-year state prison sentence. Fortunately, I was released from parole early for collegiate scholarship and compulsive attendance in 12-step meetings. Since then I have become responsible and accountable for my actions, which I wasn't previously capable of.

Addicts have an automatic denial system, especially when it comes to their addiction or when they've been accused of something. Most of the more than two million inmates in our country's prisons are innocent ;)

Before I went to prison, my querulous old friend Jack called me on the phone to explain - or whine (most drug addicts are chronic whiners) about being arrested for a burglary that he didn't commit. He carried on for five minutes about the injustice of it all. The whole time he was ranting on, something occurred to me, so I finally asked: "Jack, why are you so outraged about this?"

"Johnny, I didn't do it! God damn them! The bastards are trying to frame me."

I calmly replied, "what about all those burglaries you got away with over the last 25 years, Jack?"

"What? Don't get carried away, Johnny. The fact is, I didn't do it. This charge doesn't have anything to do with what I did before."

He dismissed my question as ridiculous.

While I was in the county jail, I overheard the following conversation: "Ya know Frenchy, I wouldn't be here for robbin that liquor store if the damn clutch wasn't bad in that old Chevy of mine. Just as I was taking off, the motor died. I got it started, then it died again. That happened three times. By the time I made it to the corner there were red lights everywhere."

"I hear ya bro, if my old lady's mother wouldn't have turned me in, I wouldn't be here either," replied Straight Razor.

I could identify with those middle-aged bikers, because I have all too often placed the blame for my behavior outside of me. It would have been a waste of time to say, "Frenchy, you wouldn't be here for robbin' a liquor store if you hadn't robbed a liquor store." It's strange, but that obvious statement is absurd to them. So it was with me.

While having a beer on my night off in the bar where I was a bartender, one of our regular customers asked if I could get him a quarter gram of speed. I said no. Later he asked again. I said no again. However, when he asked me for the third time around one o'clock in the morning, I knew that there was some meth in the bar, so I got some for him. He was a narc. I fought the sales charge in a jury trial and lost. I took it all the way through the court of appeals, and lost that too. I was entrapped! It was not my fault! They were picking on me! The truth is, if I hadn't been selling drugs, I wouldn't have gone to prison for selling drugs. However, like Jack and those bikers, I was incapable of seeing it that way.

I was 45 years old before I made it to state prison. I had been knocking on the door, however, for twenty years. As the judge looked at my rap sheet he said, "I can't figure out why you haven't been sent to prison before." Then he looked at me and said, "I can't believe that I'm sitting here trying to talk myself out of sending you to prison now."

My rap sheet didn't have violent crime on it. Though there are a couple burglary charges and a robbery charge, they were investigation charges and didn't result in conviction; in fact, they didn't get past the arraignment or preliminary hearing stage. Most of my offenses were drug and/or alcohol related. I believe that's why judges were hesitant to send me to prison. But by the time this judge viewed my rap sheet, there were 40 charges that took up several pages. As it turned out, I am glad he sent me to prison.

A few months after I arrived on the prison yard, there was an experimental program starting called Project Change. It was a nine-week education and therapy program designed for pre-release inmates. On the flyer was a request for interview. I knew that I would never terminate parole successfully unless I refrained from the use of drugs and alcohol, so I filled out the request form and interviewed for a place in the program. I only wanted to remain abstinent for as long as my parole lasted, then I planned on returning to life as I knew it before I was incarcerated - a fun- loving, dope-fiend party animal.

When I was tending bar prior to going to prison, two of my friends used to come in and drink soda. "What's up with this, Jerry?" I asked.

"I'm on parole. If I don't give my PO any dirty tests or I don't have any brushes with the law, I'll get off parole early." Jerry and Lisa both got off parole 13 months after their releases, so I was determined to do the same.

I was accepted into Project Change six months prior to my release date. Since the program was just starting, they needed to fill the dorm that was allocated for the program. Later, only inmates in their last 60 days were eligible. About a month after getting into the program, I got a clerical position with Project Change. Never having used a computer, I found an inmate in the education department who tutored me until I was familiar with the word processing program on CDC's Apple computers. Once I was proficient, I typed questionnaires, work sheets, and other classroom material, much of it gleaned from Hazeldon recovery books. We held classes five days a week in the TV room, and part of the dorm was also converted for classroom activities.

Another reason I volunteered, was for the fringe benefits. Project Change students were allowed go to chow first, and they would be first in line for commissary and linen as well as mail call. I'm surprised that more inmates didn't volunteer, if for no other reason than the fringe benefits.

The letters I was receiving from Lynda, my 21-year-old daughter, even prior to my enrollment in Project Change, were motivational and rife with 12-step clichés and jargon. She seemed genuinely happy being clean and sober. I was not much of a father to my daughter and even less of a son to my mother. I had caused them more anguish than I could ever hope to make up for; However, once I started digesting all the literature I was typing and reading, and started taking a sincere interest in the Project Change program, I started feeling the inevitable guilt associated with the wreckage of my past. I found myself seriously considering a life without drugs and alcohol, rather than just a temporary abstinence until I got off parole. I started to really want it, not for me, but for my family. After Lynda started reading my letters, rife with 12-step clichés and jargon, her return letters were so full of hope, encouragement, and happiness, that I became that much more determined to stay clean. She and my mom were so proud of me that I absolutely couldn't let them down after everything I'd put them through.

A mother's love knows no bounds in many cases. When my mom died, my aunt said, "Johnny, your mother idolized you. To her, the sun rose and set on you. There was nothing or nobody more important to her than you." My mom continued enabling me after her death. The inheritance she left provided me with enough money to finance two graduate degrees and enough for me to live comfortably since then. She went to her grave providing for the little boy she idolized. Today, I idolize her for giving me such unconditional love. She never lost faith in me. She loved me as much when I was drinking and using drugs as she did when I was a kid or after I got clean and sober.

In Project Change we were taught that we had a disease that was chronic, progressive, and fatal. Chronic because it never goes away, progressive because it keeps getting worse, and fatal because it often kills people. We also learned about family dynamics such as co-dependency, and we learned about the addictive personality, barriers to intimacy, anger management, and a special focus on relapse prevention. We did role playing in preparation for saying no. We covered a lot of the material that I encountered later as an intern at McAlister Institute in San Diego where I was doing field experience for my Master's degree. Project Change worked for me. Within four months I believed that I had recovered from a seemingly hopeless case of mind and body. I was certain that I would not drink or use drugs anymore. However, the fact is, even among those who are certain they will not drink or use drugs anymore, most of them will anyway. So it was with me.

Kathy, one of the teachers in Project Change, recognized that I had academic ability and suggested that I go to school when I was released. I said something like, "Yeah, yeah, sounds like a good idea," but I wasn't serious and she could see that. She approached me on the matter several times, practically nagging. Finally, I started giving it some serious consideration. I knew that I was going to be living with my mom again when I got out. She was on her last legs, and I wanted to take care of her for as long as she had left. I figured going to school would keep me busy with homework when I was at home. Besides, I could be of help to my mom and at the same time be doing something for myself. When Kathy heard me talking this way, she started believing that I might be serious.

In Project Change I learned that if lasting change is going to take place, one has to monitor and discipline their thought processes; therefore, if I was going to remain abstinent when I was released, I was going to have to change my thinking. As it was, almost every waking moment was spent thinking about either the bar where I was a bartender, how much fun scavenging at the dump was, the people I drank and used with, and all the women I slept with. I came to realize that being in a recovery oriented environment and having this stinking thinking going on in my head at the same time, was like having someone pushing me away and saying "come here" at the same time. I had to ask myself, how can intrinsic recovery take place with such a conflict?

All the great leaders throughout history have taught the principle that our life is the result of our thoughts. Buddha said, "A man's life is the direct result of his thoughts." Solomon said, "As a man thinks in his heart so is he." Happiness comes from happy thoughts, that's another reason why I was relatively happy when I was drinking and using drugs (or maybe I choose to only remember the good times). Success comes from successful thoughts, failure from failing thoughts, etc. So it's hard to deny, that our lives are controlled by our thinking.

Our minds have two parts: a conscious part and an unconscious part. The 'depth' component of Depth Psychology is the unconscious part. The conscious part is what we think and reason with, but the unconscious part controls bodily functions such as breathing, blood circulation, digestion, etc. It never sleeps and is working all the time. It's like a computer. It takes in data and processes it. It has a memory of everything that has ever happened to us, from the day we were born to the present moment. It is non-judgmental. It doesn't know what is good or what is bad. It doesn't care whether the thoughts come from us or from others. If we don't take the effort to program it positively, our unconscious will take directions from other people or from the environment or from our own self talk.

I use to wonder why I didn't always get what I wanted or why I couldn't do certain things. Perhaps I was sending negative messages to my unconscious, or maybe it picked up negative inputs from those around me. My dad always said that I was too easily influenced by my friends. I was.

One of the tenets of the Project Change program was: If our lives are not what we want, we have the power to change it. We change it by changing our thoughts, which are programmed to our unconscious.

So, I invented a method to change my thinking: I simply decided that I would *shoo* my old thoughts away, and replace them with different thoughts. I did this quite literally. With my hand in a swishing motion by my ear, I shooed the recurring thoughts away and started thinking other thoughts. Walking around the big yard shooing thoughts away in that manner, I could tell by the looks I was getting from fellow inmates that I was being viewed through jaundiced eyes. A nut case, I'm sure, they must have thought. I didn't care. I was on the road to a new life without drugs and alcohol. At first it took me a long time to remember to shoo the recurring thoughts away, so I only did it two or three times a day. As time passed, however, I started doing it more often, and then even more often, until I was doing it a lot - maybe 20 or 30 or even 40 times a day. That's when I was getting so many of the weird looks from other inmates on the yard. After awhile I discovered that I wasn't doing it as often. It started going back the other way. As time went on I did it less and less because I wasn't thinking the old thoughts as often anymore. I had replaced them with new thoughts. And then . . . guess what? After about three or four months I had exorcized all those old thoughts by replacing them with thoughts of what I really wanted to be doing and where I really wanted to be when I got out. I visualized myself in NA meetings, and I visualized myself in college classrooms. I also visualized spending time at home taking care of my mom, which of course, served as further impetus to remain clean and sober. How could I be a comfort to my mother at the end of her life if I was still drinking and using drugs? Eventually, staying clean had become the very most important thing in my life, more important than having fun, even more important than my daughter and mother. Without total abstinence, what good would I be to them? They may have been my incentive for getting clean, but staying clean finally became my top priority.

A couple months before my release date, Kathy volunteered to help me with the tedious financial aide paperwork so I could get the federal Pell Grant when I was released. I received the financial aide paperwork and she helped me with it like she promised. I was 45 years old and was going to be a college student again. I tried twice in the early '60s, both of which were failures, so I came to accept that I wasn't college material. And maybe I wasn't . . . then.

My daughter became clean and sober while I was doing time in the county jail - about a year before I went to prison. She still has the letters I wrote to her during that time, as well as the ones I wrote from prison. After reading over them, I am amazed at all the fatherly advice I was giving her. Some of it was actually sound, but most of it was from a refractory and hedonistic loser with an inflated male ego. One thing was consistent in those letters, however. I never failed to tell her how proud I was of her and how much I loved her. If nothing else, she grew up knowing she was loved. And that, I believe, is the reason she is the epitome of motherhood to my two grand children today.

Letters she wrote to me was recovery oriented, and she mentioned several of my dope-fiend friends who were showing up in AA meetings. It was comforting to know that I was going to have friends at meetings when I got out, but since I considered myself more of a drug addict than an alcoholic (I never thought of alcohol as a drug anyway), I planned on attending NA meetings. I eventually resolved to attend both.

Today I own the home I grew up in and I have earned a few university degrees culminating with a Ph.D. Having a doctorate, owning my home, and having my car, truck, and camper paid for are not really the things that make me happy. The closeness I share with my daughter and grand children make me happy. Thinking about the time I spent caring for my mom before she died makes me happy. But could I have sustained the happiness I had during childhood, adolescence, and through most of my drug and alcohol use had I not stopped?

No.

Why?

I will answer that by quoting a paragraph written above:

> In my opinion, happiness is part of a temperament that is innate. Of course, life's circumstances can alter that, but I believe that the basic temperament is static. If trauma doesn't strike, and we have

had a stable and loving foundation in early childhood, most of us are capable of handling most of life's encumbrances. That's my opinion, anyway.

It is highly unlikely that I could have handled the mental, physical, and emotional encumbrances resulting from continued drug and alcohol use. I learned early in recovery that becoming responsible and accountable for my actions is a cornerstone of a life well lived.

Foreword

My doctoral dissertation, *Scumbag Sewer Rats: Criminalized Male Drug Addicts and the Trickster Archetype* served as a foundation for my 2008 book, *Scumbag Sewer Rats: An Archetypal Understanding of Criminalized Drug Addicts*. In the chapter of that book entitled "Addiction, the Disease Concept, and Recovery" I borrowed philosophical ideologies from the 12 steps in the recovery section. In this book, however, I've eliminated most everything previously gleaned from the philosophies of 12-step programs so that the alchemical approach to recovery can stand alone on its own merits. In 2012 my memoir *Addict to Academic: Recovery from 30 Years of Drug Addiction* was published. Hopefully, those books, as well as this one and my website at www.JohnSmethers.com, will be an inspiration to others and their friends and/or families who don't believe that there's redemption and recovery for seemingly hopeless drug addicts.

I've used some of the same quotes and references in a few of the papers in this book; therefore, when reading a quote from another author that's been quoted in a previous paper, no lack of understanding in the content of the paper will be lost by skipping over it. In most cases, I've italicized the quotes to help identify repeated ones.

To contact the author:

John E. Smethers, Ph.D.
904 S. Second Ave,
Barstow, CA 92311
USA

Tel: 760-256-8266

www.JohnSmethers.com
email: gwakwa@gmail.com

CHAPTER ONE

Thinking Outside of the Box

Chemical dependency has been beaten like a dead horse. There are causal theories from a genetic predisposition to various theories of learning, which has contributed greatly to a social construction of reality - an area that needs to be re-visioned. Discussed here will be psychological and depth psychological perspectives concerning cause by using analogy, opinions and history. There is a galaxy of treatment methods, various forms of education, self help and scare tactics for prevention. Considerable emphasis on psychotherapy will be examined. Finally offered will be some depth psychological ideas that might help look at this phenomenon in light rather than shadow.

Woodman (1982) is convinced that;

> The same problem is at the root of all addictions. The problem being different in each individual. The problem, whatever that may be, presents itself differently in different people. Overeating, alcoholism, gambling, sex, drug addiction, etc., are all likely symptoms of an underlying cause. Some of these causes may never be known. Others should be further investigated (p. 9).

Woodman also suggests that many of us, despite gender, are addicted because we have been driven to specialization and perfection by our patriarchal culture (p. 10). Obsession is at the root of perfection. An obsession is a persistent or recurrent idea, usually strongly tinged with emotion, and frequently involving an urge toward some kind of action, the whole mental situation being pathological. The roots of fear can also be pathological.

Without going into the multitudinous causes of fear, it is often considered a legitimate reason to lean on something for emotional support. If not properly bonded, for example, fear will most likely manifest in some way. This fear being unconscious, there is not a way

19

to intervene. "The mother," says Woodman "who is in this situation herself because of her own heritage, cannot give her baby the strong bonding to the earth that the mother grounded in her own instincts can (p. 15)." Fear is often anger in disguise, and anger often produces rebellious behavior.

Rebellion encompasses various types of behavior, which of course, include criminality and/or addiction. Substance abusers are characteristically thought of as rebellious. What causes rebellion? A patriarchal society can cause rebellious behavior in women. Authority figures are often accused of creating rebellious behavior in both men and women. Rebellion can also be looked at as Otherwise: ironically, recovery can be viewed as a form of rebellion against addiction. Therefore, rebellion does not have to be negative. Rebellion can result in healing. Depth psychology is often thought of as rebellious–we and them, the familiar and the Other, right and wrong, etc. This form of rebellion is spiritual, and spirituality is an entity that needs to be developed. This form of rebellion invites change; in fact, it seeks it. Change is the only evidence of growth.

Part of a letter is published in *Pass It On* (1984) from Bill Wilson (cofounder of Alcoholics Anonymous), to Carl Jung. The letter went on to tell Jung how the message reached Bill at the low point of his alcoholism; it described his own spiritual awakening, the subsequent founding of A.A., and the spiritual experiences of its many thousands of members. As Bill put it: "This concept [spiritual experience or spiritual awakening] proved to be the foundation of such success as Alcoholics Anonymous has since achieved. This has made conversion experience . . . available on an almost wholesale basis" (p. 383).

Spiritual experiences can be life changing. Though William James wrote about spiritual experience in *The Varieties of Religious Experience*, Carl Jung introduced it to Bill Wilson and it has since changed the lives of thousands of people in Alcoholic's Anonymous as well as all of the other 12-step programs that's sprung up since. Oracular guidance is also a spiritual experience. Oracular consciousness has to be developed over time; therefore, if enough time is not devoted in developing it, what may be interpreted as oracular guidance may in reality be another unknown influence.

"Give me a sign, God!" How often have people, in one way or another, sought guidance this way? However, what if one does not believe that God exists? The trigger for addictive behavior is often pulled by stress or life events resulting in looking to the divine for guidance. Seeking oracular guidance might also pull this trigger. According to Skafte (1997) "To receive an oracle is to receive guidance, knowledge, or illumination from a mysterious source beyond the personal self"(p. 3).

Dr. Skafte proposes "that 'the shadow' may appear in unexpected places when the oracle is sought" (p.136). Personality traits and genetic idiosyncrasies are omnipresent. As is the shadow archetype, the dark side of our psyche. Relying too much on oracular guidance can lead to a road that is not conducive to spiritual needs or healing. Something as unlikely as a butterfly flying into a neighborhood tavern, could set into motion a possible solution for a problem. Taking the butterfly's flight into the bar as an oracular sign post, one could meet an old drinking buddy that he or she hadn't seen in a long time. Thinking the "oracle" has again provided guidance, a recurring dependence on alcohol could follow a drinking spree in the bar. In how many other ways can the "imaginal" cause problems? Transitions from an objective orientation to the imaginal should be approached carefully, especially the chemically dependent in recovery who's often unconsciously looking for excuses to return to active drug and/or alcohol use.

Traditional clinical treatment models in the west are numerous, and these models have been treating various forms of mental illness for over a century. Jung said;

> Psychiatry is a stepchild of medicine. All the other branches of medicine have one great advantage: the scientific method. In all other branches there are things that can be seen and touched, physical and chemical methods of investigation to be followed (C.W. 3, par.320).

Psychiatric treatments, including treatments for chemical dependency, were founded on the medical model. How effective has that been? How often have they considered culture? Not nearly enough, because if one thinks about it, culture has a monumental influence says Cushman (1995):

Nothing has cured the human race, and nothing is about to. Mental ills don't work that way; they're not universal. They're local. Every era has a particular configuration of self, illness, healer, technology; they are a kind of cultural package. They are interrelated, intertwined, interpenetrating. So when we study a particular illness, we are also studying the conditions that shape and define that illness, and the sociopolitical impact of those who are responsible for healing it (p. 7).

Shulman (1997) says;

Western healing systems for mental illness are 'ill' because they are suffering from a one-sided gerontomorphy that needs to be corrected. Behind the glass walls of our observation posts, we are concerned more with watching, recording, and diagnosing than with relating (p. 203).

James Hillman (1976), in *Re-Visioning Psychology*, believes;

...that many modern methods of psychotherapy want to retain the spirit of analysis but not its soul. They want to retain the methods and forms without pathologizings. Then the doctor can become a master, and the patient is metamorphosed into a pupil, client, partner, disciple - anything but a patient (p. 70).

Defining depth psychology would be fruitless as an antecedent to what follows because of its multi-definitional makeup. After all, a depth psychological perspective could well be an irrational one. Hillman (1983) quotes Freud as saying "in all countries into which psychoanalysis has penetrated it has been better understood and applied by writers and artists than by doctors" (p. 3). Freud was not referring to addiction, of course, but that statement does suggest that maybe scientific theories and treatment concerning substance abuse should be examined from those who are not so *supposedly informed* on the subject. Perhaps present ideas of irrational will be tomorrow's ideas of rational.

Those submerged in the scientific method often scoff at anything Otherwise because they have set the standard for what is the supposedly

22

logical existence. Cushman (1995) explains that;

> Psychologists might dress in white coats, work in what is called a 'laboratory,' and refer to their work as science, but what they are unintentionally doing is using the approved practices of their era to carry on a disguised moral discourse to justify a particular view about what is the proper way of being (p.333).

Jung, who was himself submerged in the scientific method for a long time said;

> ...while immense progress has been made in cerebral anatomy, we know practically nothing about the psyche, or even less than we did before. Modern psychiatry behaves like someone who thinks he can decipher the meaning and purpose of a building by a mineralogical analysis of its stones (C.W. 3, par. 324).

The tremendous complexity of psyche led Jung to believe that attempts to formulate a comprehensive theory of the psyche was not possible. Therefore, as vast as the psyche is, the points that Freud and Jung makes are well taken.

Psyche may well use addiction as a pedagogical tool in the same way it may use mental illness as a pedagogical tool. It is common for those with mental disorders to turn to helping others with similar problems by becoming therapists, and it is also very common to find recovered addicts and alcoholics in the field of addiction as counselors.

Whether we utilize oracular guidance, consider culture, study areas of the Other, develop a metaphysical knowledge base, use symbols as metaphors, pray for guidance, or dis-identify with the status quo and challenge authority, what is most important in life is to be happy, whether our means of getting there is accepted by others or not. If one is happy in the presence of animals, why not benefit from them? McElroy (1996) does:

> Blessed with a wide assortment of spectacular human and animal mentors, I have always received the counsel I needed if I just waited and watched long and closely enough. Animals have

been masters at bringing me examples of courage and joy that cannot be surpassed. Judging from the many responses I received about animals as healing mentors, it's evident that many people agree (p. 83).

Active imagination can be a transcendent function - a living connection to the collective unconscious. Images can be used as metaphors to be used as guide posts. Therefore, why not, in some way use another unconventional activity - the waking dream? With practice, the waking dream can be of service. Watkins (1977) describes "the attempt to dream while awake, itself paradoxical, involves one in a number of paradoxical states, actions, and attitudes." Watkins says "this opus creates a directionality away from the perceptual and the material, to the imaginal and the psychological" (p 14).

Music, art, sculpture, sports, education, various spiritual paths, plants, animals, nature, play, children, helping others, reading, computers, crafts, meditation: all these things and more, with what has been previously discussed are not mutually exclusive. So, could the waking dream, for example, in combination with the Internet, find a way into psyche to alleviate the persistent intrusion of addictive thinking?

These last few concepts of light rather than shadow is probably not possible for many of those who live in the world of addiction, but for those who are willing to change old ways of thinking and doing, into new ways of thinking and doing, just about anything is possible.

Chapter One References

Alcoholics Anonymous World Services, Inc. (1984). *Pass it on: The story of Bill Wilson and how the A.A. message reached the world*. New York, NY: Alcoholics Anonymous World Services, Inc.

Cushman, Phillip. (1995). *Constructing the self, constructing America: A cultural history of psychotherapy*. Reading, MA: Addison-Wesley Publishing Company, Inc.

Hillman, James. (1976). *Re-Visioning psychology*. New York, NY: Harper Perennial.

Jung, Carl. (1960). *The psychogenesis of mental disease*. New York, N.Y: Pantheon Books.

McElroy, Susan Chernak. (1996). *Animals as teachers & healers*. Troutdale, OR: New Sage Press.

Shulman, Helene. (1997). *Living at the edge of chaos: Complex systems in culture and psyche*. Daimon Verlag: University of Chicago Press.

Skafte, Diane. (1997). *Listening to the oracle: The ancient art of finding guidance in the signs and symbols all around us.* New York, N.Y.: Harper Collins Publishers.

Watkins, Mary. (1976). *Waking dreams*. Woodstock, CT: Spring Publications.

Woodman, Marion. (1982). *Addiction to perfection: The still unravished bride*. Toronto, Canada: Inner City Books.

CHAPTER TWO

Numinous Aspects

A Broken Bond

After having attended 12-step meetings for more than eleven years, I still didn't understand what members meant when they'd mentioned spiritual experiences. Since then, I did a research study with AA members to find out, and have consequently come to understand that there are many forms of spiritual experience. Spiritual experience and the numinosum are synonymous, and they can range from a simple coincidence to burning bushes and bright blinding lights. Since coming to a relative understanding of the numinous, I realize that I have had such experiences.

When I was twenty-two years old, I received a phone call from Lynda, my junior high school sweetheart. She was in town and at the bus station. When we hung up the phones, we started walking toward one another and met in the middle. This was the beginning of a three-year relationship that produced our beautiful daughter.

My dad was ill during this time. As decadent as this might sound, my focus lied more with my new found love than with my father's declining health. He was eventually hospitalized, and his previously arrested cancer had reared its ugly head again. The last time Lynda and I visited him in the hospital, he was very weak. For some reason the doctor informed me that they'd given him fifty milligrams of secobarbital (a very high dose I remember thinking). Then he suggested that I leave and let him get some rest - that I could visit the following morning. I reluctantly complied. As I was walking out of the hospital room, I looked back, and my dad appeared to be summoning me back with his eyes. I couldn't tell for sure, for his face was so riddled with pain. I wish I'd stayed, in spite of the doctor's suggestion. Lynda and I spent the night in my car in the parking lot.

During the night I awoke with a start - sitting up in the seat with my eyes wide open. I hadn't ever awoken in that manner before or since. I looked around, looked up toward his room, and then laid back down and went to sleep.

On the way to my dad's hospital room the following morning, at the nurses' station, a nurse informed me that my dad had passed away during the night. If I had considered the possibility of his dying that night, we would have spent his last hours together, but how was I to know? - *mors certa, hora incerta*, death is certain, the hour uncertain.

Did I awake at the instant that my dad passed away? I don't know. I didn't check the time. This occurred in 1968. I believed then and I believe now that this was either a synchronous or a synchronistic event; however, I wouldn't have used those words at that time. Nor did I see this event as a spiritual experience, but these circumstances subtly affected me for the rest of my life. Whereas I continued to sustain a basically Cartesian world view at the time - *hoc opus*, this is the difficulty, from that point on I wasn't as closed-minded about it. You might say that it made a formerly closed door ajar. Today, however, I see this experience as spiritual. Like anyone else, I have had other coincidental things happen in my life, but I would not have considered them spiritual experiences. However, a much more common route, especially for me, to the numinosum, was through altered states of consciousness.

Altered States of Consciousness
Wanting to feel good is visceral. In whatever form we choose, whether it's religious revivals, speaking in tongues, going on vision quests, meditating, sky-diving, ejaculating or doing drugs - it can still be thought of as numinous. In one way or another, from time immemorial, drugs have played a role in religion, from the ancient Mayans and African tribal beliefs to modern day Shamanism. Often, the drugs used were seen as opening the gateway to the "spirit world" and only spiritual leaders would use them on behalf of their people. Corbett (1996) explains;

> The imagery of the shaman's journey is fairly similar in its themes in different parts of the world because the shaman

experiences directly those categories of the imagination which are archetypal. To reach them, the shaman enters or evokes the necessary state of consciousness through ritual, or by means of the enactment of myth, which allows access to the spirit world (the transpersonal levels of the unconscious). Techniques such as fasting, drumming, dancing or hallucinogens all produce intense affective arousal, expansion of the spectrum of ordinary perception and a submersion or suspension of consensual reality. Such altered consciousness is often necessary for the evocation of archetypal material (p. 125).

When we think of drugs, however, we think of the illicit ones like cocaine, heroin, and LSD, but we overlook the seemingly insignificant and socially acceptable licit drugs such as nicotine and caffeine. I only mention passively the use of alcohol in Christian rituals such as the Eucharist. However, when a Christian drinks the blood of Christ, they do not do so to the extent of oblivion. Neither does the exploration with drugs on a Shamanic level lead to pathological euphoria. It's not like the societal disturbance we see with an alcoholic or heroin addict–*aegrotat*, he or she is sick. It's the use of a drug for a constructive mental process. The difference being that one often sets out to destroy the mind whereas the other sets out to educate it.

Our society is presently saturated with the overindulgence in chemical substances. Yet, less than a hundred years ago people were drifting blissfully in the clouds of Morpheus. Morphine and laudanum were highly recommended for many ailments, as was smoking tobacco. Today the drugs may be stronger and more destructive, but perhaps their abuse is an unconscious attempt at spirituality; such as teenagers attempting to alleviate the boredom in a boring society not geared to nurture their individuality and accommodate their spiritual needs. I realize that the previous statement is hard for most people to digest, but don't judge it too harshly yet.

The use of opium goes back unofficially to the ancient cave dwellers who drew pictures of the poppy plant on the cave walls. Officially, according to a Frontline history on the Internet, it goes back to 3400 B.C.E. where it was "cultivated in lower Mesopotamia. The Sumerians refer to it as Hul Gil, the joy plant. The Sumerians would soon pass along the plant and its euphoric effects to the Assyrians. The art of poppy-culling would continue from the Assyrians to the Babylonians who in turn would pass their knowledge onto the Egyptians. In 460 B.C.E. Hippocrates, the father of medicine, dismisses the magical attributes of opium but acknowledges its usefulness as a narcotic and styptic in treating internal diseases, diseases of women and epidemics. By the 1300's opium disappeared for two hundred years from European historical records. It had become a taboo subject for those in circles of learning during the Holy Inquisition, then it resurfaced again by the Portugese in the 1500's. In 1680, English apothecary, Thomas Sydenham, introduces Sydenham's Laudanum.

Tussionex was my Laudanum. For eight and a half years I sustained a diurnal practice of writing and filling pharmaceutical prescriptions for Tussionex. Getting arrested by the police was nugatory - *malesuada fames*, hunger that urges people to crime. During those parlous years I was arrested five times on felony charges with only being convicted twice on misdemeanors. What made Tussionex a schedule three controlled substance was hydrocodone resin complex. Unlike the fugacious cocaine, it had a long duration - from eight to twelve hours (its formula has since been changed). I share the opinion with others that Tussionex was the most superior opiate drug, a virtual halcyon of euphoria. The numinosum, however, is not always upbeat and wonderful. There isn't anything spiritual about the often scabrous struggle to sustain an opiate addiction, whether it's heroin from the drug dealer or pharmaceuticals obtained by forged prescriptions.

The numinosum can be negative. When Corbett (1997) mentions Mark, Luke, Matt and Cor., when discussing celibacy, he mentioned that "the body and sexuality acted as a kind of negative numinosum" (p. 161). My body and Tussionex, acted as a negative numinosum - one that kept me going back for more despite the problems that being a drug store bandit caused. Life on a daily basis was like being under the sword of Damocles, which makes the family of opiates the most opprobrious and addictive. Hallucinogens, however - especially LSD, peyote and mescaline, are thought of as the most mind-altering and spiritual.

Concerning the origin of religion - the ancient mystery cults, Gordon Wasson (1986) shares with us;

In Antiquity people spoke of the Mystery of Eleusis, of the Orphic Mysteries, and of many others. These all concealed a secret, a 'Mystery'. But we can no longer use 'Mystery', which has latched on to itself other meanings, and most of us know the uses and misuses of this word today. Moreover, we need a word that applies to the potions taken in the antique Mysteries, now that at last we are learning what they were. 'Hallucinogen' and 'psychedelic' have circulated comfortably among the Tim Learys and their ilk, and uncomfortably among others for want of a suitable word: 'hallucinogen' is patently a misnomer, as a lie is of the essence of 'hallucinogen', and 'psychedelic' is a barbarous formation. No one who respects the ancient Mystery of Eleusis, the Soma [mushroom] of the Aryans, and the fungal and other potions of the American natives, no one who respects the English language, would consent to apply 'hallucinogen' to those plant substances. Antiquity remained silent on these plant substances, for they were never mentioned, except perhaps person to person in a low voice, by the light of a candle at night.

Wasson and others formed a committee under the Chairmanship of Carl Ruck to devise a new word for the potions that held Antiquity in awe. After trying out a number of words they came up with entheogen "God generated within," not to replace the Mystery of the ancients, but to designate those plant substances that were and are at the very core of the Mysteries (p. 30).

John H. Laney (1972) quotes La Barre expressing the following anthropological opinion: "Without a doubt [it is] the most widely prevalent present day [1947] religion among the Indians of the U.S. . . . the use of Peyote has spread from group to group until today it has assumed the proportions of a great intertribal religion" (p. 110). Laney wrote that "the movement has been referred to variously as Peyotism, Peyote Cult or Sect, and Peyote Religion. The members, themselves, know it nominally as The American Church of North America. I prefer to call it the peyote movement because of its creatively dynamic character" (p. 110). "It has also been referred to as Father Peyote, Peyote Jesus, holy food, our brother, and medicine. ("Medicine" in the Indian sense, meaning a mana substance, is capable of curing the mind as well as the body)" (p. 127).

The spiritual ambiance of the peyote movement wasn't necessarily an organized religion. "Owing probably to the strongly individual orientation of the members," says Laney (1972), "as well as to their interest in, and closeness to, the original religious experience, there is no theology in the movement, no officially formulated doctrine" (p. 112). Whereas I have not had personal experience with peyote, I've had considerable experience with LSD.

I spent roughly five years experimenting with psychedelic drugs - mostly LSD. I have fond memories of those years, without ever having experienced a bad trip. Was I a netherworld criminal who was in possession and under the influence of illegal drugs, or was I having spiritual experiences by means of nonordinary states of consciousness? According to state law, I was a firebrand - stirring up trouble and committing crimes. According to me, then, I was getting high. According to me, now, I was experiencing the numinosum through nonordinary states of consciousness. Today, I do not condone the recreational use of drugs. In fact, I advocate total abstinence, but I have to ask myself: do I regret the past? No on both counts. I believe I am the person I am today because of how I lived my life–*quantum mutatus ab illo*, changed from the person you once were. Without those psychedelic experiences with LSD, I think it's possible that there would be a part of me missing - an asset, I might add, for in some ways I can still see through those psychedelic eyes. If one wants to experience the numinosum through nonordinary states of consciousness, suicide is always an option. Not really, but there are better ways to do it. A more acceptable manner is Stanislav Grof's holotropic breathwork.

Grof (2000) shares that;

> In the last twenty-five years, my wife Christina and I have developed an approach to therapy and self-exploration that we call 'holotropic breathwork. It induces very powerful holotropic states by a combination of very simple means - accelerated breathing, evocative music, and a technique of body work that helps to release residual bioenergetic and emotional blocks. In its theory and practice, this method brings together and integrates various elements from ancient and aboriginal traditions, Eastern spiritual philosophies, and Western depth psychology (p. 183).

31

Before holotropic breathwork, Grof and other physicians discovered a number of therapeutic uses for LSD. Grof (2000) explains that;

> In the early 1960s, Eric Kast of the Chicago Medical School studied the effects of various drugs on the experience of pain in search of a good and reliable analgesic. During this study, he became interested in LSD as a possible candidate. In a paper published in 1963, Kast and Collins described the results of a research project, in which the effects of LSD were compared with two established potent narcotic drugs, the opiates Dilaudid and Demerol. Statistical analysis of the results showed that the analgesic effect of LSD was superior to both opiates. (p. 250).

That was a medical use for LSD. There are also psychotherapeutic uses. Grof continues: "The encouraging results of Kast and Collins's studies inspired Sidney Cohen, a prominent Los Angeles psychiatrist, a friend of Aldous Huxley and one of the pioneers of psychedelic research, to start a program of psychedelic therapy for terminal cancer patients." Cohen confirmed Kast's findings concerning the effect of LSD on severe pain and stressed the importance of developing techniques that would alter the experience of dying (Cohen 1965). His co-worker, Gary Fisher, who continued these studies, emphasized the important role that transcendental experiences play in the treatment of the dying, whether these are spontaneous, resulting from various spiritual practices, or induced by psychedelic substances" (p. 251). In my case, during the time that I was experimenting with LSD, the term psychedelic was suitable. However, considering the numinous benefit of those experiences now, I might endeavor to use the term entheogen. Although I haven't found the term entheogen relegated to the coca plant in any of the literature, I think that it would be suitable prior to its synthesis.

At another web site, this one sponsored by Narconon, we can find cocaine history: "Cocaine in its various forms is derived from the coca plant that is native to the high mountain ranges of South America. The coca leaves were used by natives of this region and acted upon the user as a stimulant. The stimulating effects of the drug increases breathing which increases oxygen intake. This afforded native laborers of the region the stamina to perform their duties in the thin air at high altitudes." Whereas Narconon didn't provide any dates with the above description of the coca plant, it does with the chemical synthesizing of it. Narconon shares that "Cocaine was first synthesized in 1855. It was not until 1880, however, that its effects were recognized by the medical world. The first recognized authority and advocate for this drug was world famous psychologist, Sigmund Freud. Early in his career, Freud broadly promoted cocaine as a safe and useful tonic that could cure depression and sexual impotence. Cocaine got a further boost in acceptability when in 1886 John Pemberton included cocaine as the main ingredient in his new soft drink, Coca Cola. It was cocaine's euphoric and energizing effects on the consumer that was mostly responsible for skyrocketing Coca Cola into its place as the most popular soft drink in history. From the 1850's to the early 1900's, cocaine and opium laced elixirs, tonics, and wines were broadly used by people of all social classes. This is a fact that is for the most part hidden in American history. The truth is that at this time there was a large drug culture affecting a broad sector of American society. Other famous people that promoted the *miraculous* effects of cocaine elixirs were Thomas Edison and actress Sarah Bernhart. There is a longer list of historic figures that used cocaine and other drugs, but it is not necessary to discuss them here.

Laney (1972), referring to the peyote movement, said that;

> In my experience, not only does a general lack of information exist about this movement, but a quantity of dramatic misinformation exists in its place; that it belongs somewhat to the 'drug culture', that it is a decadent, deteriorating religious form, that it is an orgiastic or ecstatic mode of primarily unconscious experience. This disparaging attitude seems to prevail even among the psychologically informed. It comes, apparently, from the same human need that expresses itself in feelings of excitement, awe, fear, fascination, or lust when faced with the mysterium. It seems actually to arise from the sense of the numinous (p. 126).

Laney was writing about Peyote, but why couldn't it apply to other drugs as well? Except for the lust, the feelings of excitement, awe, fear, and fascination when faced with the mysterium, this description resembled a brief experience I once had. At the time the ignominious injection of methamphetamine was my elixir, which have similar deleterious effects to the mind and body as the chronic and addictive use of cocaine. After having been in a sleepless imbroglio for three or four days and nights, my friend stopped her car in front of my house. When I asked her where she was going, she told me that she was going to see Billy - her ex-boyfriend. She asked if I wanted to go with her. As soon as she asked, I felt an overwhelming sense of excitement, awe, fear, and fascination. This cerebral/emotional paroxysm also had a physical quality - a throbbing, pins and needles sensation throughout my body. The most numinous part of this, maybe a fifteen second experience, was fear. I could not say "No!" and get the hell out of that car fast enough. Once I was inside of my house, I remember saying to myself something like, "Wow! What was that all about?" Pondering on the numinosity of that event afterwards, I passed if off as diminished mental capacity - a drug induced quirk coupled with sleep deprivation, *non compos mentis* - not of sound mind. I still believe that, but I also believe that I had some kind of a spiritual experience–one that I will probably never know the specific meaning or nature of. Sleep deprivation, after several days and nights of injecting methamphetamine, have sent me on a number of cerebral excursions into the numinosum - the negative numinosum, of course - a nonordinary state of consciousness is putting it very lightly.

Conclusion

Most addicts will assert that it was not their intention to grow up to be self-centered, hedonistic drug addicts and/or alcoholics. Nor was that my intention (I don't think?). I'm not sure because when I was around six or seven years old, there was something about the outlaw that was compelling and attractive to me. However, during the same time period, when my playmates and I played cops and robbers, I always wanted to be the cop. At this early age I was already beginning to develop the structure of both the *puer aeternus* (eternal boy) and *senex* (old man) archetypes into my life. These consentaneous opposites are what is at the heart of addictive personalities. Hillman (1970) explains "that the senex is a complicatio of the puer, infolded into puer structure, so that puer events are complicated by a senex background" (p. 146). Most of the research I did during the five years I was working on my doctorate concerns the *puer* and *senex* archetypes, and it is my firm belief that in the chemically dependent population of our society, this structure

34

begins to develop in childhood. It did with me, anyway.

It might appear to some that I've shone a heterodox light on the wide spread view that the recreational use of chemical substances should be avoided. This is not my intention. Hopefully, my words won't be taken officiously. In 12-step programs such as AA and NA there is an expression that explains the general human condition when people voluntarily enter recovery programs: incomprehensible demoralization. They are subjugated and they want to surrender. That was not the case with me. Unlike most 12-steppers, my life with drugs and alcohol was not incomprehensibly demoralizing. However, *quae nocent docent*, things that injure teach.

I believe I have been preordained to do something in my second life, but to accomplish it; I first had to attend a drug and alcohol school for more than thirty years in my first life. Then, in order to earn the credibility to write and teach about what I learned in my first life, I had to go to more schools in my second life. Since I've finished with the formal education of my second life, I have taught college and university courses and have written about the spiritual journey of my first life - and *that,* I think is what I was preordained to do, hence the acorn theory. Consequently, for me, my heterodox view of my first-life experiences will hopefully serve me and others well for as long as my second life lasts.

I believe my entrance into recovery efficacious, luckily keeping me from having to experience incomprehensible demoralization. Eventually, however, I would've experienced that. I might have even died–*mea culpa, mea culpa.*

Chapter Two References

Corbett, L. (1997). *The religious function of the psyche*. New York: Routledge.

Grof, S. (2000). *Psychology of the future*. Albany: State University of New York.

Hillman, J. (1970). "On senex consciousness." *Spring: An Annual of Archetypal Psychology and Jungian Thought*.

Laney, J. H. (1972). "The peyote movement: An introduction." *Spring: An Annual of Archetypal Psychology and Jungian Thought*.

Narconon. (2000). *History of cocaine*. Retrieved November 20, 2001 from http://www.cocaineaddiction.com

PBS and WGBH Frontline. (1998). *The opium kings*. In Opium Throughout History. Retrieved November 25, 2001 from http://www.pbs.org/wgbh/pages/frontline/shows/heroin/etc/history.html

Wasson, R. G., Kramrisch, S., Ott, J., & Ruck, A. P. *Persephone's quest: Entheogens and the origins of religion*. New Haven and London: Yale University Press.

CHAPTER THREE

Permanent Adolescence vs Rites of Passage

*P*uer Aeternus is Latin for eternal boy. *Senex* is Latin for old man. However, this is just one archetype - a split archetype. Hillman (1970) explains "that the senex is a complicatio of the puer, infolded into puer structure, so that puer events are complicated by a senex background." (p. 146). Explaining that the senex has a double nature, Hillman continues by saying "one characteristic is never safe from inversion into its opposite" (p. 148). So what? How does all that relate to the real world?

Since a thorough examination of the *puer* is usually incomplete without discussing its *senex* counterpart, for the sake of brevity and focus, only the *puer* will be discussed here. Both of them will be examined in the paper titled "Puer and Senex.".

Having been an inveterate alcoholic/drug addict for more than 30 years of my life, those years can be juxtaposed with the problem of the *puer aeternus*. I went to a party when I was eleven and didn't get back until I was 45 years. Indeed, the *puer* was alive and well in me the whole time. Having spent time in the Augean stables of county jails and ultimately the state penitentiary, I noticed that the *puer* population was alive and well in there too - a virtual pied-a- terre.

Most inmates are imprisoned for substance-related offenses. Kipnis reminds us that "drug offenders represent 60 percent of federal prisoners and over one-third of state and county prisoners" (p. 121). These statistics do not include the inmates who are within the walls, because of *malesuada fames* - hunger that urges people to crime: crimes committed to finance drug and alcohol use, or crimes committed while under the influence. In the netherworld of the prison yard, I found that most inmates were much like me in many ways - quite comparable to the scabrous characters whom I associated with on the streets.

Marie-Louise von Franz (2000) describes me (the *puer*) as;

> …having an arrogant attitude toward other people due to both an inferiority complex and false feelings of superiority. Such people also usually have great difficulty in finding the right kind of job, for whatever they find is never quite right or quite what they wanted. There is always 'a hair in the soup' (p. 8).

Lionel Corbett (1997), when addressing narcissism, writes that "pathological grandiosity which is needed to maintain a fragile self structure may make one depreciate the religious values of other people for the sake of self enhancement (p. 34). Not only toward religious values, I might add, but toward any values unlike their own.

Me and my puerile friends were often, to say the least, irresponsible. I am reminded of the time, under the influence of methamphetamine, I was digging holes in the desert at an old dump site. I was so preoccupied with this frivolous activity that I made a conscious decision to not go to court on a Failure to Appear charge. The Peter Pan in me wanted to play instead. According to Kiley (1983);

> Victims of the Peter Pan Syndrome can't escape irresponsibility. This trap begins as innocent, typical rebellion, but mushrooms into an adult lifestyle. A fundamental piece of the puzzle of the Peter Pan Syndrome is gross irresponsibility that spawns ineptness in basic self-care skills (p. 45).

Irresponsibility, a false sense of superiority, going from job to job, not bathing for a week at a time, and a penchant for *blandae mendacia linguae* - the lies of a smooth tongue, and building air castles are only some of the quotidian traits of the *puer aeternus*. This is not to say that *puer* traits are all negative. Gauche as the *puer* is, he is usually very affable, sanguine, well-intentioned, and good-natured. Many of his often subtle *senex* attributes also enhance the positive *puer*. His firebrand presence on prison yards, however, and his chemical dependency further exacerbates the plight of the negative *puer*. So, how might we account for such vast numbers of people in this country caught in the problem of the *puer aeternus*? One popular theory is that American youth are virtually without formal rites of passage - *hoc opus*,

38

this is the difficulty.

To ignore rites of passage or dismiss them as trivial or unnecessary rituals is as ridiculous as denial being a river in Africa. Gleaned from The Stanton Peele Addiction Web Site, it is stated that;

> In a 1980 article in the American Sociological Review and a 1984 article in the Journal of Studies on Alcohol, where two sociologists at the University of Syracuse, Barry Glassner and Bruce Berg, investigating Jewish drinking in a large upstate New York city because they believed that traditionally low Jewish alcoholism rates had increased over the years. Of the Jewish people the sociologists actually interviewed, none had ever had a drinking problem. Investigating all reports by activists in the Jewish community who had announced a growing alcoholism problem, Glassner and Berg could not actually locate one Jewish alcoholic. Accepting at face values all such reports led to calculation of an alcoholism rate of about one-tenth of one percent among Jewish adults.

Wow! Could it be that a bar mitzvah is responsible for this? Probably - at least where drugs and alcohol are concerned. However, judging by reports from the Jewish community, they do have other addictions such as overeating and anorexia. According to the National "Jewish Press," Ross (April, 1986) reports that there are seven to 10 thousand Jewish inmates in the United States. That is not very many compared to the two million Americans that Kipnis (1999) reports who are behind bars (p. 170). Under the aegis of the church, could initiatory rites of passage account for the absence of the *puer* in Jewish culture? If so, one could be compelled to investigate rites of passage in other cultures.

"The term initiation," as defined by Eliade (1958) "in the most general sense denotes a body of rites and oral teachings whose purpose is to produce a decisive alteration in the religious and social status of the person to be initiated" (p. x). The closest I came to being elevated from a child to something more than a child, was my entrance into junior high school. Without so much as a caveat from the elementary school level, what followed came as a radical social change. In what seems now like an almost overnight transformation, I went from a pleasant grade school boy to an acerbic junior high school rebel without a cause: from playing on the monkey bars to getting drunk at Friday night football games; from wrestling with schoolmates on the playground to gang fights with rival Mexican gangs after school - riotous, no doubt, as the Germanic berserkers of antiquity; from playing hide-and-go-seek with girls to whisking them out of the movie theater to kiss and fondle them - not unlike Theseus carrying off Adriadne (p. 109); from recess to smoking in the bath rooms during breaks; from evenings home with parents to malicious mischief in the community with my buddies. It could be argued that there is a nexus between our malicious mischief and the spirit of initiation. My friends and I felt compelled to prove ourselves to each other, so we acted out an incredible amount of destructive behavior in the process. This alchemical coniunctio, from boy to wacko, also involved more subtle anomalies. Discussing initiation in Tierra del Fuego, Eliade mentions that "a frequent custom is that of giving the novice a new name immediately after his initiation" (p. 28). Soon after my nascent arrival into junior high school, one of my new friends tagged me with the nick name of Little Richard. I remained Little Richard for the rest of my first life. My first life being my drug and alcohol years; my second life being my post drug and alcohol years; my pre life being a rather short childhood.

The closest I came to a formal initiation ceremony during puberty was my sixth grade graduation ceremony, elevating me to junior high school status. This happened at about the same age as the bar mitzvah does in Jewish culture. Being unfamiliar with the bar mitzvah and what their ordeals entails, I believe it is safe to assume that there are painstaking lengths gone to for some kind of enduring conversion. Eliade (1958) says that among the Australian Yuin tribe "the first initiation ceremony, comprising the separation from the women and the ordeal by fire, is thus complete. From that night on, the novices share only in the life of the men"(p.8). Indeed, the elevation to junior high school with its incumbent social status, seemed to suddenly sever an emotional attachment to my parents, and created a different kind of emotional attachment to my newly acquired friends - friends, I might add, some of whom I kept for more than 30 years. In discussing the secret society of the Bakhimba in Mayombe, Eliade shares that "the initiatory ordeals continue from two to five years" (p. 75).

When considering my adolescence, I could say that my initiatory ordeals, or rather my initiatory gradations, also continued for years; thereby eventuating the problem of the *puer aeternus*. After my elevation to junior high, I could not bear the interminable passage of time to arrive at Xvarnah - that light of glory that the magical age of 16 brings, when that golden driver license can be attained. I took a driver education class at 15 and a half and avoided the 16-year-old driver license requirement by legalizing my driving privilege with an instruction permit. This legal manipulation empowered me to drive a car if I had a licensed driver with me. It also empowered me to drive a motor-driven cycle without any supervision; therefore, I talked my parents into allowing me to spend my savings on a Cushman Eagle motor scooter. Wa la, I attained independent mobility. Not only did my social status go up another notch, but my mobility put me in contact with the higher echelons of the streets. The Los Diablos motorcycle gang even took me under their wing. I had arrived! My blissful state of Xvarnah, however, was short-lived. Later that summer I was arrested and jailed for curfew. Two weeks later a friend and I were arrested for stealing milk off a porch after staying out all night drinking. A few months after that I got my first of six DUI's. When I went to court, my coveted driver license was revoked before I got it. Consequently, my dad took away the motor scooter and I found myself immobile and distraught.

Can my entrance into junior high school be considered a rite of passage? Can my driving privilege be considered a rite of passage? Probably not - at least not in the traditional sense. However, it is my contention that these were different kinds of rites of passage. Not having adequate formal guidance - I guided myself, which is common, and has been for a long time. The lack of parental control, of course, exacerbates the situation.

Eliade (1958) says that;

> Even if the initiatory character of these ordeals is not apprehended as such, it remains true nonetheless that man becomes himself only after having solved a series of desperately difficult and even dangerous situations; that is, after having undergone 'tortures' and 'death,' followed by an awakening to

another life, qualitatively different because regenerated (p. 128).

By the time I was socially established in junior high school, I had been through various tortures and been awakened into another life by suffering with hangovers, sporting black eyes and bruises from fighting, getting in scooter and car accidents, enduring punishment for indiscretions at school, and continually having to endure the wrath and retribution of my officious parents for my refractory behavior. It could be said that I was tortured when I was metamorphosed from the archetypal innocence of a butterfly into a nasty old caterpillar (etymologically cater comes from tomcat and pillar comes from plunderer). By the time the caterpillar summer was over, my rebellious lifestyle had been firmly established. This new and parlous life - this self-will run riot, continued until I was 45 years old. Graduating from high school and turning 18, then turning 21 were still further entrenchments, but they were really gradatory inevitabilities compared with the junior high school awakening that established an eonian lifestyle. I did not experience rites of passage in the way they were experienced in the mystery religions or in any other traditional way.

"Modern man," explains Eliade (1958);

> ..no longer has any initiation of the traditional type. Certain initiatory themes survive in Christianity; but the various Christian denominations no longer regard them as possessing the values of initiation. The rituals, imagery, and terminology borrowed from the mysteries of late antiquity have lost their initiatory aura (p. 132).

However, there is a more formal movement of initiation going on in society today under the guise of another name - hazing.

At a web site sponsored by Education Week, Walsh (September 6, 2000) reports that;

> Almost half the high school students responding to a national survey said they had been subjected to activities that fit a broad definition of hazing to become members of sports teams, cheerleading squads, gangs, and other groups. The study by

researchers at Alfred University in New York, released last week, is described as the first serious academic research into initiation rites at the high school level. Some of the results surprised even the authors. For example, the survey showed that 24 percent of students joining youth church groups faced hazing. The study's authors, expecting little hazing in that category, almost didn't include it in the survey. Among all survey respondents, nearly one out of four students was required to engage in substance abuse, such as participating in drinking contests. And 22 percent were subjected to activities the researchers defined as dangerous hazing not involving substance abuse, such as stealing, inflicting pain on themselves, or being physically abused.

Drinking contests, daredevil fighting, stealing to fit in, etc., were the callow activities I participated in during my pubescence - a temporary *modus operandi* that I consider initiatory, even though I wasn't being forced to do it. If I hadn't, however, then I would have been alienated or suffered some other type of consequences. Durkheim (1995), discussing tattooing, states that "it is true that, among the Arunta, the design thus made does not always and necessarily represent the totem of the novice" (p. 116). It astonishes me today that I willingly endured such excruciating pain incurred from tattooing, macho-acting as though it wasn't painful at all. I now consider this *non compos mentis* - not of sound mind. Durkheim, however, shares that "Preuss was the first to become aware of the religious role that is ascribed to pain in the lower societies" (p. 317). Of course we did not conceive ourselves as doing anything religious or even spiritual, but our tattoos were always symbolic to the interests of our group.

Walsh's article went on to describe in detail the various forms of hazing that I am not inclined to include here. The original study he quotes from is available at the previously mentioned web site.

Conclusion
Obviously, our youth in this country is now, and has for a long time been ripe for some kind of formal rites of passage, and since we don't seem to feel it is necessary to incorporate it into our culture - they are. Like solicitous parents, we should take heed of *magnum bonum* - the

great good, of the bar mitzvah in the Jewish community and do a commensurate service to our pubescent population by supplanting independent hazing practices. This may be too idealistic. Such an achievement would, indeed, be an improvement for society's ills. Whether it is hazing, addiction, or any type of aberrant behavior, most of us know that what we're doing is not conducive to a productive life - *video meliora proboque, deteriora sequor*, I see the better course of action and I approve of it, but I follow the worse course. Here is a parable to this Latin phrase.

"According to Webster's Dictionary," says Ellis (1985);

> Mumpsimus is an error obstinately clung to. The word comes from the story of an old priest who, for thirty years, had conducted services using the word mumpsimus, a substitute for the correct Latin word *sumpsimus*. One day, when his error was finally pointed out to him, he replied, 'I will not change my old mumpsimus for your new sumpsimus.' (p. 106).

The bottom line: Without a significant rite of passage, much of our youth will remain adolescent in behavior and attitude far into adulthood - *puer aeternus* forever.

Chapter Three References

Corbett, L. (1997). *The religious function of the psyche*. New York: Routledge.

Corbin, H. (1989). *Spiritual body and celestial earth: From mazdean Iran to shi'ite Iran*. Princeton, NJ: Princeton University Press.

Durkheim, E. (1995). *The elementary forms of religious life*. New York: The Free Press.

Eliade, M. (1958). *Rites and symbols of initiation: The mysteries of birth and rebirth*. New York: Harper& Row Publishers.

Ellis, D. (1985). *Becoming a master student: Tools, techniques, hints, ideas, illustrations, instructions, examples, methods, procedures, processes, skills, resources and suggestions for success*. Rapid City, SD: College Survival Inc.

Hillman, J.(1970). "On senex consciousness." *Spring: An Annual of Archetypal Psychology and Jungian Thought*." Dallas, Texas: Spring Publications.

Kiley, D. *The Peter Pan syndrome: Men who have never grown up*. New York: Dodd, Mead & Company.

Kipnis, A. (1999). *Angry young men: How parents, teachers, and counselors can help "bad boys" become good men*. San Francisco, CA: Jossey-Bass.

Miller, D. (1973). "Achelous and the butterfly: Toward an archetypal psychology of humor." *Spring: An Annual of Archetypal Psychology and Jungian Thought*. Dallas, Texas: Spring Publications

Peele, S. (11/12/2001). "Would legalization of alcoholic drinks to minors decrease or increase underage drinking?" In The Stanton Peele Addiction Web Site. Retrieved December 18, 2001 from www.peele.net/faq/childdrink.html

Ross, R. (April, 1986). *Three nation umbrella org. to aid Jewish prison inmates, families. In National Jewish Press*. Retrieved December 30, 2001 from www.rickross.com/reference/Jewpris5.html

von Franz, M. *The problem of the puer aeternus*. (1988). Toronto, Canada: Inner City Books.

Walsh, M. (6 Sept. 2000). "Hazing is widespread, student survey shows." In Education Week. Retrieved December 15, 2001 from www.edweek.org/ew/ewstory.cfm?slug=01haze.h20

CHAPTER FOUR

Archetypes and Stereotypes

> The "eternal child" in man is an indescribable experience, an incongruity, a handicap, and a divine prerogative; an imponderable that determines the ultimate worth of worthlessness of a personality. C.G. Jung (CW 9i, par. 300)

Because of the growing and changing prison population in this country, I will reiterate statistics of the presence of an archetype. Personal observation on the prison yard has brought to my attention that most of my fellow inmates did not fit the prison stereotype that popular media portrays. My main point is to show the existence of a much larger population of chemically addicted inmates, who fit the archetype of the *puer aeternus*. Those same types of people I associated with for more than twenty-five years, many of whom, never spent any prison time whatever.

From the roaring twenties through the 1950s various forms of the media have characterized a prison stereotype that includes gangsters, sociopaths, convicts and ex-convicts. Presented here will be a discussion about that prison stereotype, drawing from Babyak and Gilligan, followed by a discussion of an archetype - the *puer aeternus* - that is descriptive of present-day inmates. Aaron Kipnis will provide the reasons for this. With help from Erich Fromm, also discussed here will be two types of aggression that will differentiate the old stereotype and the *puer*. Nakken, von Franz, Yeoman, et al, will compare the puer aeternus with the addicted population of our country's prisons.

The Prison Stereotype
The convict, the sociopath, and the gangster stereotypes are not mutually exclusive. Their acerbic personalities are often described as hardened, violent, racist, devoid of compassion, destructive, and untrustworthy. It is no wonder that so many people in our society want to keep them locked up for their turpitude.

Humphrey Bogart and Fredric March portrayed escaped convicts in a classic nail-biter in The Desperate Hours where they held a terrified family hostage. Robert DiNero has portrayed similar figures in films such as Goodfellas, True Confessions, and Cape Fear. Whereas their roles are fictional, there are those in real life who are found on the front pages of daily newspapers, in magazines, biographies, case studies, newscasts, and documentaries about serial killers, pedophiles, rapists, cannibals, sadists, and many other people who have committed atrocities, and these people have always and will continue to be housed in prisons.

Thomas Gaddis provides an excellent example. He was the author of a book entitled *Birdman of Alcatraz* about Robert Stroud, which is what inspired the 1962 movie of the same name. The Hollywood portrayal made him look like an American folk hero with his scientific discoveries in medicine and his compassion for birds, but in the real world of the state prison system he was quite different from the movie portrayal.

Jolene Babyak (1994) paints a more accurate picture of him: on "November 1, 1911, Stroud struck Henry in the back with a knife. As Henry ran, Stroud got off a few more thrusts. A physician reported that Henry received seven stab wounds in his back, shoulder, upper arm and buttocks, one of which penetrated the pleural cavity." Stroud later admitted that "he had intended to kill Henry and regretted being unsuccessful." It was Bird Man's intention to kill two other prisoners too. Stroud was also a homosexual who "proudly called himself a 'pederast,' a man who prefers sex with boys" (p. 62). The MMPI confirmed a previous diagnosis of a "profoundly and significantly disturbed personality, a 'psychopathic deviate' who was impulsive and paranoid–the perfect profile of a sociopath" (p. 252).

Gilligan (1996) quotes Dennis X who intended to "gouge out his eyes, cut off his ears, cut out his tongue, cut off his penis and testicles, and then stuff all these up his anus. He was unable to complete that project only because the knife broke. Following the murder, "Dennis X experienced no feelings of guilt or remorse" (p. 80).

The violence described above is what Fromm (1973) considers

47

malignant aggression: "cruelty and destructiveness, is specific to the human species and virtually absent in most mammals; it is not phylogenetically programmed and not biologically adaptive; it has no purpose, and its satisfaction is lustful" (p. 25).

The majority of inmates in this country do not fit the scandalous prison stereotype just described. Kipnis (1999) reports studies done by the Prison Activist Resource Center that lists the top ten reasons for Californians entering prison today:

1. Possession of a controlled substance

2. Possession of a controlled substance for sale

3. Robbery

4. Sale of a controlled substance

5. Second-degree burglary

6. Assault with a deadly weapon

7. Driving under the influence

8. First-degree burglary

9. Petty theft with a prior conviction

10. Vehicle theft

Clearly, violent crime is practically absent (p. 176).

According to Kipnis, drug offenders represent 60 percent of federal prisoners and over one-third of state and county prisoners (p. 121). Considering those percentages, let us examine the top ten reasons for Californians entering prison, which is likely to be similar across the nation. Numbers one, two, four, and seven are directly substance-related. However, how many of the people incarcerated for numbers three, five, eight, and nine were acquiring money to support a habit?

And how many of number six' assaults (the only one involving destructive behavior) were committed while under the influence? That would be hard to determine, as would the correlation existing between number ten and substances.

The *Puer* Archetype

This archetype is not shrouded in violence and destruction. *Puer aeternus* is Latin for "eternal boy" and used in mythology to refer to a child-god who is forever young. Psychologically it refers to an older man whose emotional life has remained at an adolescent level - a puerile nature.

Nakken (1988) offers a timeless description of how adolescents usually live for the moment. He posits;

> That practicing addicts also live for the moment, using emotional logic. Emotionally, addicts act like adolescents and are often described as adolescent in behavior and attitude. After all, many issues they struggle with are the same issues that face adolescents. The difference is that addicts stay trapped in an adolescent stage as long as their disease is in progress (p. 16).

Marie-Louise von Franz (2000) agrees: "In general, the man who is identified with the archetype of the puer aeternus remains too long in adolescent psychology; that is, all those characteristics that are normal in a youth of seventeen or eighteen are continued into later life" (p. 7). Von Franz was not including the chemically addicted, however, since her lectures were presented in 1959-60 in Zurich. At that time, even here in the United States, drugs were not a big problem yet, but there has been a big problem with alcohol addiction for a long time all over the globe. Apparently, it did not occur to her to correlate alcoholics with the problem of the *puer*.

Impatience is a classic symptom of the chemically-dependent. In meetings of Alcoholics and Narcotics Anonymous everywhere members talk about their struggles with impatience. In the big book of Alcoholics Anonymous "The Man Who Mastered Fear" wrote, "at long last I am doing the kind of work I have always wanted to do, but never had the patience and emotional stability to train myself for" (p. 284).

Again von Franz agrees:

> And then something absolutely classic happens, namely, the gesture of impatience. That is typical for the puer aeternus! When he has to take something seriously, either in the outer or the inner world, he makes a few poor attempts and then impatiently gives up (p. 30).

Yeoman (1998) finds other traits that's characteristic of the *puer*.

> Peter Pan and Captain Hook share many characteristics. Both have difficulty relating to others; they are isolated and self-centered; each is motivated by a lust for power and control and each fears the passage of time with the inevitable changes and transformations it occasions (p. 16).

That passage also describes the chemically-dependent. Most will agree that getting along with or relating to alcoholics and drug addicts are, at best, difficult. If one attends NA or AA meetings for very long, selfishness and self-centeredness are themes inevitably heard around the tables. Control is also omnipresent. In addiction there is the seductive illusion that a person can be in absolute control.

Yeoman quotes Satinover concerning the *puer*:

> This missing sense of identity, or of oneself as a cohesive whole, results in disquieting feelings of fragmentation and worthlessness. It motivates the puer's pursuit of the ecstatic 'high' - in drugs, alcohol, sex, sport and daredevil escapades - that transcends the outer conflict or inner depression which threatens fragmentation (p. 24).

To suggest that violence or aggression is absent among this part of the prison population would not be realistic. In addition to the malignant aggression mentioned earlier, Fromm talks about another type of aggression: "This defensive, 'benign' aggression is in the service of the survival of the individual and the species, is biologically adaptive, and ceases when the threat has ceased to exist" (p. 25). The prison environment is conducive to a certain amount of violence. Self preservation warrants it. Gilligan believes that "the very conditions that occur regularly in most prisons may *force* [italics mine] prisoners to engage in acts of serious violence in order to avoid being mutilated, raped, or murdered themselves" (p. 163).

In explaining how normal people usually outgrow immaturity and irresponsibility, Kiley (1983) reminds us that;

> *Victims of the Peter Pan Syndrome have the opposite problem. They can't escape irresponsibility. This trap begins as innocent, typical rebellion, but mushrooms into an adult lifestyle. A fundamental piece of the puzzle of the Peter Pan Syndrome is gross irresponsibility that spawns ineptness in basic self-care skills (p. 45).*

The Peter Pan syndrome of the *Puer aeternus* has a co-dependence with the prison system when it comes to enabling irresponsibility. In my 1992 magazine article, I share my prison experiences by explaining that;

> Inmates are well provided for, having little, if no responsibility for themselves. Our clothes and linen were cleaned for us every week - all we had to do was drop it off and pick it up; they provided our meals for us - all we had to do was wait in line and eat; we had a big yard to play on - a weight pile where we could flex our muscles, show off, and be macho. We built reputations, status, and respect from our peers by controlling the drug and alcohol flow, managing moneymaking schemes, and having our subordinates do our dirty work. Drugs were plentiful on the yard, and pruno (homemade wine) was easily made. At that time, every three months we could have money and material things (a package) sent to us from home. If we were married, we could even spend the weekend in a bungalow with our wives and relieve ourselves sexually. In maximum security prisons that have rooms (cells), we could enjoy watching our own color television (p. 3).

Conclusion
For many years the popular media has characterized the prison

51

stereotype as violent, dangerous, and desperate, as Gilligan and Babyak have explained. By providing Kipnis' statistics of the current prison population, we see the emergence of a new population - those who are incarcerated for substance-related charges. Not being within the scope of this paper to explain the reasons why, I've offered ample feedback from von Franz, Kiley and Yeoman to indicate the nature of this large percentage of the prison population. To be sure, many ex-cons - including me - do not want the opprobrium associated with the prison stereotype.

Chapter Four References

Alcoholics Anonymous World Services, Inc. (1976). *Alcoholics anonymous*. New York: Alcoholics Anonymous World Services, Inc.

Babyak, Jolene. *Bird Man: The many faces of Robert Stroud*. (1994). Berkeley, CA: Ariel Vamp Press.

Fromm, Erich. (1993). *The anatomy of human destructiveness*. New York: Henry Holt and Company, Inc.

Gilligan, James. *Violence*. (1996). New York: Vintage Books.

Jung, C.G. *The archetypes and the collective unconscious*. (1959). New York: Pantheon Books.

Kiley, Dan. *The peter pan syndrome: Men who have never grown up*. New York: Dodd, Mead & Company.

Kipnis, Aaron. *Angry young men*. (1999). San Francisco, CA: Jossey-Bass Books.

Nakken, Craig. *The addictive personality*. (1988). San Francisco, CA: Harper & Row Publishers.

Smethers, John. (1995). "Prison-the day care center." *Pleiades Magazine*, Vol 11, No. 9.

von Franz, Marie-Louise. *The problem of the puer aeternus*. (1988). Toronto, Canada: Inner City Books.

Yeoman, Ann. *Now or neverland: Peter Pan and the myth of eternal youth*. Toronto, Canada: Inner City Books.

CHAPTER FIVE

Puer and Senex

This paper and the previous one have some of the same material and quotes from various authors, but the premise of each paper is different. The previous paper focused on prison stereotypes and archetypes, whereas, the *puer* and *senex* is the focus here. In the previous paper, I separated inmates into two groups: the old prison stereotype and the new prison population who personify the *puer* and *senex* archetypes. In motion pictures, Humphery Bogart, James Cagney and many others have since portrayed gangsters, sociopaths and convicts. These categories are not mutually exclusive. Their stereotypical image is often described as hardened, violent, racist, devoid of compassion, destructive, and untrustworthy, among other things.

Most inmates in this country nowadays do not fit the scandalous image described above. Aaron Kipnis (1999) reports studies done by the Prison Activist Resource Center that lists the top ten reasons for Californians entering prison today. The rest of the country likely has comparable statistics. Among those criminal charges, violent crime is practically absent. (p. 176). According to Kipnis, "drug offenders represent 60 percent of federal prisoners and over one-third of state and county prisoners" (p. 121). Taking into consideration that many of the remaining inmates are also there indirectly related to drugs and/or alcohol, then the statistics probably rise dramatically, which gives the netherworld of our prison yards a population of men personifying various archetypes - focusing here on the callow *puer aeternus*.

The *pueri*, on the streets, is not shrouded in violence and destruction in and of itself, but often their aggression is exacerbated by their drugs of choice. While incarcerated the puerile inmate's violent behavior is influenced by his environment. Erich Fromm (1992) talks about this type of aggression: "This defensive, 'benign' aggression is in the service of the survival of the individual and the species, is biologically adaptive, and ceases when the threat has ceased to exist." (p. 25). The prison environment is conducive to a certain amount of violence. Self preservation warrants it. Gilligan (1996) believes that "the very conditions that occur regularly in most prisons may force prisoners to engage in acts of serious violence in order to avoid being mutilated, raped, or murdered themselves (p. 163). During their imprisonment many continue to use drugs and sustain addictions. Drugs are as easy to obtain on the inside of the walls as it is on the outside. Stan Grof (2000) writes that "Among archetypes that show important connection with addiction, that of *puer aeternus* with its varieties of Icarus and Dionysus, seems to play an important role." (p. 112).

Nakken (1988), describing the nature of the chemically dependent, has also partially described *puer* psychology:

> *Adolescents usually live for the moment. Practicing addicts are also living for the present moment, using emotional logic. Emotionally, addicts act like adolescents and are often described as adolescent in behavior and attitude. After all, a lot of issues addicts struggle with are the same issues that face adolescents. The difference is that addicts stay trapped in an adolescent stage as long as their illness is in progress. (p. 16).*

Marie-Louise von Franz, James Hillman, Ann Yeoman, Jeffrey Satinover, and Dan Kiley, et all, have described many other parallels between the chemically dependent and the puer. As Moore (1991) describes:

> The puer strives for vertical flight. His feet are not on the ground. He has little patience for development, for working things out. Puer wants things done immediately, and his impatient idealism finds the sage counsel of the senex establishment an anchor and a weight. As the street pueri like to say: "It's a drag!" (p. 191)

The traits these authors report of the *puer*, describe me prior to and upon arriving at the guiding center at the California Institute for Men in Chino.

Shortly after my arrival in Chino, I approached a prison guard on the yard and asked if he knew where I could find a book to read. He looked at me in disgust and said, "do I look like a fucking library to you?" I looked at him and said emphatically, "Hey!" He then turned back to me and said just as emphatically, "What!" I then softened and replied, "Ya know . . ., it doesn't cost a thing to be nice." I caught him completely off guard. He looked away, then looked back at me, then looked away again. He looked like he didn't know what to say or do. Finally he said "You're right, I shouldn't have spoken to you like that." Then he told me what I asked of him in the first place.

Defined by Sharp (1991) in the C.G. Jung Lexicon "puer aeternus is Latin for 'eternal child,' used in mythology to designate a child-god who is forever young; psychologically it refers to an older man whose emotional life has remained at an adolescent level." In Latin, *puer* can refer to male or female; however, the female counterpart to the word *puer* is the Latin word *puella*, meaning "girl" or "maiden." *Senex* is the Latin word for "old man," comparable to "senior." However, it can also mean old woman. Hillman (1989) describes personifications of the *senex* as "in the holy or old wise man, the powerful father or grandfather, the great king, ruler, judge, ogre, counselor, elder, priest, hermit, outcast and cripple." (p. 208).

I will add parole and probation officers, police officers and prison guards to the list. The rift between inmates and prison guards is widely acknowledged. Also well known is the similar rift that exists between parolees and their parole officers. The rift continues between police officers and criminals, which include gang bangers and the chemically dependent, et al. The quotidian, solicitous existence of these groups is spent looking over their shoulders or looking in the rear-view mirror. After a few scabrous years in recovery from drugs and alcohol, I finally stopped doing all that.

The *senex* archetype originates in the Greek god Saturn-Kronos, (Kronos is the Greek word for time). Hillman (1970) explains:

> Saturn presides over honest speech - and deceit; over secrets, silence - and loquacious slander; over loyalty, friendship - and selfishness, cruelty, cunning, thievery and murder. He is the just

executioner and the criminal executed; *the prisoner and the prison* [emphasis mine]. He is retentive but forgetful; slothful and apathetic but rules the vigil of sleeplessness. His eyes droop with depression, apathetic to all events, and they stare inconsolably open, the super-ego eye of God taking account of everything. He makes both honest reckoning and fraud. He is God of manure, privies, dirty linen, bad wind - and he is cleanser of souls. Senex duality presents moral values inextricably meshed with shadow; good and bad become hard to distinguish. Because of the inherent antitheses, a morality based on senex-consciousness will always be dubious. No matter what strict code of ethical purity it asserts, there will be a balancing loathsome horror not far away, sometimes quite close - in the execution of its lofty principles. Torture and persecution are done in the best of circles for the best of reasons: this is the senex. (pp. 154, 155).

Another aspect of this, shares (1967) Jung,

..is the dual nature of Mercurius and his characterization as senex and puer. The figure of Hermes as an old man, attested by archaeology, brings him into direct relation with Saturn - a relationship which plays a considerable role in alchemy. Mercurius truly consists of the most extreme opposites; on the one hand he is undoubtedly akin to the godhead, on the other he is found in sewers. Rosinus (Zosimos) even calls him the terminus ani. In the Bundahish, the anus of Garotman is 'like hell on earth.' (C.W. 13, par. 269).

Age did not apply between me and the prison guard, for I was older than he; therefore, we can look at him as the *senex* and me as the *puer*. Or, perhaps he was also a *puer* working in the capacity of a *senex*. Hillman (1970) says "that the senex is a complicatio of the puer, infolded into puer structure, so that puer events are complicated by a senex background." (p. 146). Explaining that the *senex* has a double nature, Hillman continues by saying "one characteristic is never safe from inversion into its opposite." (p. 148). Perhaps we can view me and/or the prison guard with the term *puer senilis*, for "our puer attitudes are not bound to youth, nor are our senex qualities reserved for age." (Puer Papers, p. 10).

It has often been said that there is a fine line between the nature of criminals and the nature of law enforcement officers. They are very much alike in many ways. The same can be said of parole and probation officers and prison guards, but I will use the words of a retired police officer to demonstrate my point.

I attended a public meeting of the Claremont Forum where four panelists were giving talks about prison, each coming from their personal or professional backgrounds. The first panelist was Gil Contreras, a former Los Angeles police officer - rampart division, who was at the time working as a journalist. Gil's *mea culpa* promulgated a *modus operandi* that generally does not get talked about - especially in public and on videotape. As a law enforcement officer, his credentials are impressive, which includes being a qualified gang and narcotics expert. My purpose here is to demonstrate a parallel between cops and criminals, sometimes using parts of Hillman's previous quote concerning Saturn to help elucidate *puer et senex.*

Gil said there is a universal "cop culture." He said that during his reign as a police officer, they functioned very much as hunters. For example, they would act like victims to get criminals to commit a crime against them, then other officers would jump out of the bushes, beat them up, arrest them and take them to jail, *lupus est homo homini* - man is wolf to man, i.e., men prey on one another. "Saturn presides over honest speech - and deceit." Police officers, deceitful as they often are, also perform honorable service, for "he makes both honest reckoning and fraud."

Gil stated that "we actually didn't mind shooting people at all." Saturn "is the just executioner and the criminal executed." We know that the life of a cop often ends in a paroxysm of violence. We also know that gang life on the streets often ends in violent death. The violence of each group (and the similarity of their thinking) is congruent with their respective codes of ethics, *silent leges inter arma* - the laws are silent amid arms. According to Morwood's (1998) Dictionary of Latin Words and Phrases, "Cicero argues that, when one's life is threatened by violent plots and the laws have been reduced to silence, one has the right of self-defense in any way possible." (p. 167).

Cops make their jobs personnel, devoting their lives to it; therefore, the shady side of their jobs they view as exculpatory - they do it with impunity. Gil said that "cops act very much like gangs: each have uniforms, each have their own codes they talk in, each have belief systems about right and wrong - both being very rigid, each tends to be uneducated - most street cops are high school graduates or GEDs, and each are closed societies - viewing people that are not a part of it as outsiders. "Outsiders," stated Gil, "don't need to know that we're out there hunting criminals." Most outsiders are not aware of the augean stable that resides in many police departments.

The peccant behavior of one of Gil's partners was that of arbitrarily starting fights for various reasons, one of them being to see what his partner would do. In other words, to see if they could trust Gil not to report his partner's behavior to their superiors. Gil said that during his law enforcement years, he knew that the things he was doing were wrong but he felt inviolable. However, we have to ask ourselves, how much good did he do over the years he spent as a police officer? "*Senex* duality presents moral values inextricably meshed with shadow; good and bad become hard to distinguish. Because of the inherent antitheses, a morality based on senex-consciousness will always be dubious. No matter what strict code of ethical purity it asserts, there will be a balancing loathsome horror not far away, sometimes quite close - in the execution of its lofty principles." Gang bangers have the reputation for being bad, but human nature tells us that there is inherent good in all people; therefore, we have the same dichotomy as we do with police officers.

"When debriefing," Gil said, "we often drank alcohol until five o'clock in the morning." Police officers have a high rate of alcoholism and drug addiction. Since cops are usually hired right out of the community, finding prospective police officers that have not experimented with drugs and alcohol is hard, so hiring them is often an imbroglio. Drugs and alcohol are part of cop culture. Drugs and alcohol are also a part of gang culture.

Police officers also have a high suicide rate. "His eyes droop with

58

depression, apathetic to all events, and they stare inconsolably open, the super-ego eye of God taking account of everything." Unfortunately, teenage depression and subsequent suicide are one of the highest causes of death among that age group.

So, "puer and senex are always together," Frankel (1998) reminds us, "yet it is very common for one to be split off from the other. To grasp this potential for splitting, let us take a closer look at the phenomenology of the *senex*:

> Kronos, is son of Uranus (the sky) and Gaia (the Earth). In response to the tyranny of his father, Kronos castrated him and took over his rule. But Kronos quickly became as brutal as his father and worried that one of his children would depose him in the way he himself had deposed his father. To prevent this from happening again, he swallowed his children one by one as they were born. Only Zeus escaped and eventually, through a war with his father, took his place. (pp. 183, 184).

Gil's former website conveyed more of his concerns. He said that his experience as a cop is not unlike the experience of other cops nationwide, *haud ignota loquor* - I say things that are not unknown.

Between the summer of 1960 and the latter part of 1991 when they released me from parole, there was scarcely a time when I was not either doing time, pending court, paying fines or restitution, doing community service, or on probation or parole. During that time it was my experience that county jail and prison guards, and parole and probation officers in many ways parallel the above description of police officers.

I would like to conclude by drawing on psychiatrist Stan Grof's (2000) perinatal perspective. He says that traditional medicine denies that the child can consciously experience birth and they claim that this event is not recorded in memory. Grof states that the traditional medical view is that only a birth so difficult that it causes irreversible damage to the brain cells can have psychopathological consequences. (p.29). In dispute, Grof emphasizes

59

That the amount of emotional and physical stress involved in childbirth clearly surpasses that of any postnatal trauma in infancy and childhood with the exception of extreme forms of physical abuse. There is convincing evidence amassed that biological birth is the most profound trauma of our life and an event of paramount psychospiritual importance. It is recorded in our memory in minuscule details down to the cellular level and it has profound effect on our psychological development. (p. 31).

Stan Grof, et al, has taken patients through the rebirth experience. They used LSD and other psychedelics in the past, but more recently they accomplish this through holotropic breathwork. "The work with holotropic states shows that the perinatal level of the unconscious plays a critical role in the genesis of phobias." (p. 77). There's a host of other disorders caused by the birth trauma that have been successfully treated by using these methods.

Reliving this stage of birth is one of the worst experiences we can have during self-exploration that involves holotropic states. We feel caught in a monstrous claustrophobic nightmare, exposed to agonizing emotional and physical pain, and have a sense of utter helplessness and hopelessness. Feelings of loneliness, guilt, the absurdity of life, and existential despair reach metaphysical proportions. A person in this predicament often becomes convinced that this situation will never end and that there is absolutely no way out. (pp. 42, 43).

To equate this with the prison experience, Grof tells us that "we can experience identification with prisoners in dungeons, victims of the Inquisition, and inmates of concentration camps or insane asylums." (p. 43). Archetypally, perhaps inmates are feeling a perinatal sense of entrapment with "absolutely no way out." Addiction is also a prison, often with absolutely no way out. Prison guards are also in prison - the difference being that they go home every day. Maybe the prison guard and the inmate have unconsciously chosen to be safe within the walls of prison, much like the safety of the womb before that violent, traumatic entry into the world. It's my contention that there's not much difference between the inmate and the prison guard, police officer, or the parole and probation officer. Many years ago if someone had suggested this theorem to me, I would have scoffed at the absurdity of it. *Omnia mutantur, nos et mutamur in illis* - all things are in the process of change, we also are in the process of change among them.

Conclusion

Considering my personal experience with prison and its constituents, I am afraid I have inadvertently lain bare a prejudice that I am trying to reverse, for at one time I hated most authority figures. It is unfathomable to me today to think what the world would be like without police officers. In my quest for self-exploration, it is my view that the world is flawed but capable of being improved, and this places me firmly in the tradition of meliorism - that middle ground between optimism and pessimism.

Another archetype personified by criminalized drug addicts is the Trickster, which is too lengthy to be included here. The *puer/senex* and trickster archetypes characterize addictive behavior (in all societies and during any time period of human experience), which is what make them archetypes. For more information on the trickster, go to my website at www.ScumbagSewerRats.com or my book, *Scumbag Sewer Rats: An Archetypal Understanding of Criminalized Drug Addicts.*

Chapter Five References

Frankel, Richard. (1998). *The Adolescent Psyche: Jungian and Winnicottian Perspectives*. New York: Routledge.

Fromm, Erich. (1973). *The Anatomy of Human Destructiveness*. New York: Henry Holt and Company.

Gilligan, James. (1996). *Violence: Reflections on a national epidemic*. New York: Vintage Books.

Grof, Stanislav. (2000). *Psychology of the future: Lessons From Modern Consciousness* Research. Albany: State University of New York Press.

Hillman, James. (1970). "On senex consciousness." *Spring: An Annual of Archetypal Psychology and Jungian Thought*. Dallas, Texas: Spring Publications.

Hillman, James. (1989). *A blue fire*. New York: Harper and Row Publishers. Jung, C.G. (1967). Alchemical Studies. Princeton, N.J.: Princeton University Press.

Kipnis, Aaron. (1999). *Angry young men: How parents, teachers, and counselors can help "Bad boys" become good men*. San Francisco, CA: Jossey-Bass.

Moore, T. (1994). "Artismis and the puer," in *Puer Papers*. Dallas, Texas: Spring Publications.
Morwood, James. (1998). *A dictionary of latin words and phrases*. New York: Oxford University Press.

Nakken, Craig. (1988). *The Addictive personality: Understanding compulsion in our lives*. San Francisco, CA: Harper and Row Publishers.

Sharp, Daryl. (1991). *C.G. Jung lexicon:A primer of terms & concepts*. Toronto, Canada: Inner City Books.

CHAPTER SIX

Alchemy and the 12 Steps

What is alchemy?

Many of us are drawn to the mysteries of the past to enlighten the quality of the present. Mythology, astrology, the tarot, runes, and I-Ching have drawn the interest of many in recent years, and is being enjoyed and utilized in fresh and innovative ways. Ancient wisdom imbued by myths, legends and symbols can generate transformation, and transformation is what alchemy is all about. More commonly known as the art of turning base metal into gold, few people realize what a vast philosophical foundation this early science has. Alchemy is a process that continues to grow and expand, offering deeper understanding, awareness, and a profound potential to change your life. This fountain of ancient wisdom has nourished seekers of spiritual enlightenment throughout the ages.

The first material of alchemy, the prima materia (primal material), is a base substance known to all yet recognized by only the astute. The outward form of the prima materia must be destroyed because it is pure chaos. Treatment of the prima materia in the alchemical vessel by heat leads to its death, a moment known as the *nigredo*, or blackening. With a methodical treatment and heat, the prima materia *whitens*, indicating that the elixir is perfected in its first degree, a moment known as the *albedo*, or whitening. To attain the gold-promising tincture of the sun, further treatment is necessary until the elixir reddens, which is referred to as the *rubedo*. There is also a *citrinitas*, a yellowing in the ancient process, but it isn't used in most texts that delineates the alchemical process, especially the psychological and philosophical treatises, and more specifically to the process of the alchemical process of recovery from addiction.

Alchemy transforms consciousness, which is the project of depth psychology. When non-Jungians study Jung's concept of the transference, they are often struck by how heavily it draws on alchemical symbolism. I won't be relying much on alchemical symbolism in my approach, but transference is always an issue between sponsors and the people they sponsor in 12-step programs.

In a way, sponsorship is practicing psychotherapy without a license. Unlike therapists, however, sponsors aren't paid for it. Members of 12-step programs have been practicing psychotherapy without a license since the 1930s under the guise of sponsorship. With this model of sponsorship, transformation through the alchemical process can be achieved using a modified version of the steps.

History
Alchemy has a history stretching back at least 2,500 years and has been practiced in Eastern, Arabic and Western societies. Historically, alchemists were more interested in the chemical techniques, others in the philosophical aspects, and some saw alchemy as a path to the true meaning of Christianity, while others saw the possibilities of producing medicines and other concoctions. A more comprehensive coverage of alchemy can be found online with any search engine.

12-step programs, however, have a much shorter history, originating in 1935 when two alcoholics, Dr. Bob Smith and Bill Wilson, met. From two people to millions just in AA, not to mention all the other types 12-step programs, the 12-steps are now universally known. Carl Jung, a pioneer depth psychologist, had a key role in the founding of AA, and he's also written extensively on the psychologically and spiritually transformational aspects of alchemy.

Alchemical formula for recovery
The mercurial spirit of the prima materia is known as chaos. The newcomer to recovery certainly fits that description. It is the job of the alchemist to kill the prima materia and in the process the prima materia is turned into the blackening state of nigredo. This sets the stage for a transformation - the first conuinctio (conjunction).

The first conuinctio begins when the ego (consciousness) discovers the reality of the unconscious and makes an effort to pay attention to it. If recovery is being sought for intrinsic purposes, then the ego has acknowledged an unconscious need; therefore, the first conuinctio is the transformation from the dregs of active addiction to the *clamor* of abstinence, and I emphasize clamor because at this time abstinence is often as chaotic as active addiction. This part of the transformation is tentative and unstable.

The second conuinctio is the transformation from abstinence to recovering. What was previously only an ideal becomes a living reality. This stage of recovering can be thought of as the whitening of the albedo - the ego having reached a new level of being. The addict (which includes the alcoholic), at this new level of being, now has hope.

The third conuinctio is the transformation from recovering to recovered. This can take anywhere from about six months to many years, and sometimes it never happens. There are those too who even stay in the abstinence stage (albedo) indefinitely, which is referred to as white-knuckling it, and a regression can happen during any stage of transformation. There's also those who return to the chaos of the negredo - that prima materia that existed prior to the recovery process, which can be translated as relapse.

Application
The main purpose of sponsorship is to guide the newcomer through the 12-steps. There are many approaches to this.

When a newcomer asks someone to sponsor them, that someone sets the parameters of the sponsorship. Here's a crude example: I might ask a newcomer to squat down and quack like a duck around an entire football field. If he tells me where to stick the football field, then I won't sponsor him. Outlaw motorcycle gangs and college fraternities do similar things. Anyway, his first homework assignment will be for him to read some literature on alchemy, then give me a report on it.

The Twelve Steps
The first conuinctio has gotten the newcomer to abstinence and to meetings - if recovery is being sought for intrinsic purposes, then the ego has acknowledged an unconscious need. Before the transformation to the second conuinctio can occur, he needs to get a sponsor and start working the steps. There is no specific schedule for working the steps,

and with this model the steps are modified.

Those seeking recovery with a sponsor using the alchemical method, are most likely the ones who have issues with the traditional Christian sky-God - that is, the agnostics and atheists. The 12-steps are fraught with the word God, so I have reformatted the wording where the word God usually appears. I have made other minor changes in wording and process to conform to my approach.

1. We admitted we were powerless over addiction - that our lives had become unmanageable

This is the first step of recovery. While still in the nigredo state, the newcomer must admit he has a problem. He will actually be working this step when an alchemical oriented sponsor interviews him as a candidate for sponsorship, and this is when the sponsor determines whether the prospect's reasons for being in the program are intrinsic or extrinsic. If he is in the program as a result of a nudge from the judge, or to get his wife back, or for any other extrinsic purpose, then they can't go any farther until the sponsor is convinced the prospect is there for himself. If the prospect is there for himself, then he is no longer a prospect, but a sponsee. The sponsor will then give the following series of questions as a homework assignment.

Have you seriously damaged your relationships with other people because of your addiction? If so, list the relationships and how you damaged them. If other people have told you how you have hurt them, write down what they said. Describe times and ways that you have significantly neglected or damaged relationships with your loved ones in order to indulge in your addiction. Describe any illnesses caused by your addiction. Describe incidents when you expressed inappropriate anger toward other people. Describe embarrassing or humiliating incidents in your life related to your addiction. Describe attempts that you have made in the past to control your addiction. How successful have they been? Do you feel any remorse from the ways that you have acted in your life? If so, explain. Describe any irrational or crazy set of events that have happened since you began your addiction. Did you rationalize this behavior? If so, in what way? Have you avoided people because they did not share in or approve of your addictive behavior? If so, list these people and situations. Can you pinpoint when your life began to become unmanageable? If so, describe that period of time and what was happening. Is there one incident or insight that made you realize that your life was unmanageable? If so, describe it in detail. How would you summarize the powerlessness and unmanageability of your life in the face of your addiction?

2. Came to believe that a power greater than ourselves could restore us to sanity

The sponsee can use whatever he wants as a higher power, but for the sake of this paper, we'll use the group, since this approach will be used primarily by non-religious addicts. Once the sponsee really believes the group (or whatever he's adopted as a higher power) can restore him to sanity, the sponsor will begin to see the blackening contents of the alchemical vessel starting to whiten. The sponsor will then assign the following questions as homework.

What was the religion that your family of origin practiced? List the positive and negative aspects of your family's religion. Recall some of your best friends from childhood or adolescence. Describe what you liked best about them and what they liked best about you? Do you think that these qualities have any relationship to a higher power? Explain. Describe any dreams that you've had about a higher power or God, and what they mean to you.

3. Made a decision to turn our will and our lives over to the care of the group

This step doesn't mean for the newcomer to turn his will and his life over to the care of a sponsor or the group. It does mean, however, that he will make a decision to, if that's what it takes. It also means that he will take suggestions such as attending 90 meetings in 90 days. By monitoring his attendance, and listening to what the sponsee has to share in meetings, when 90 days has passed, the sponsor will have an idea whether he is serious or not. At the sponsor's chosen time, since all sponsees respond differently to treatment, the following questions will be given as homework.

What are your greatest fears about giving up temporary control over your life to the group? Do you think that the group can help handle your life better than you have? How do you feel overall about turning your life over to the group? In what ways will you keep up the process of turning your life over to the group? Possibilities include going to religious services, 12- step meetings, meeting with others in recovery, writing a journal, service to others, meditation, reading, physical exercise, contacting your sponsor or engaging in psychotherapy. Describe who or what you trust and to what degree. What changes do you expect to make and how will this look in specific detail?

4. Made a searching and fearless moral inventory of ourselves.

Steps four and five are major action steps. Step four is an inventory which sets the stage for the fifth step. This inventory should include not only the deep dark immoral secrets of hedonistic and ignominous turpitude, but also the more admirable traits that have often gone unnoticed. Homework assignment:

Have you had any broken relationships? If so, describe them and how they hurt others or you. Describe any grudges, anger or resentment that you have over these relationships. Have you ever behaved self-righteously? Explain. Was this justified? What caused you to begin your addictive behavior? Describe situations, feelings, events or people that were a part of your life just before your addictive lifestyle started. Have you held grudges? Did you get revenge? If so, explain and include whether or not someone else was hurt. Describe the faults that you most detest in others, and if you have any of these traits yourself?

5. Admitted to our sponsor or to another human being the exact nature of our wrongs

All of those despicable things the newcomer has done during his addiction have been kept a secret and needs to be shared with another human being. If he or she doesn't wish to share things with their sponsor, then they should find another sponsor. Most sponsors, during their addiction, have done most of the things that their sponsees have done, so there's really not a valid reason to refuse to disclose past behavior. Homework assignment:

After working through the fourth step questions, what do you realize about your limitations and capabilities? Describe what it was like sharing the fifth step. How did you feel before, during, and after the process? Are you glad that you've done this?

Usually by this time the sponsor will have already witnessed the contents of the alchemical vessel transform from the blackening of the nigredo to the whitening of the albedo. The sponsor will discuss with him at what point of the alchemical process he's at - if he has internalized his recovery as an alchemical process and recognizes the importance of the transformation of the second conuinctio, then they can continue their journey of transformation. Hopefully the sponsee has internalized the death of his old self and the birth of the new. The benefits of the fourth and fifth steps, if the sponsee is successful, are the completion of the second conuinctio - the whitening of the alchemical vessel has turned red and is therefore in the rubedo phase.

Twelve-step programs recognize various lengths of being clean and sober. In an alchemical recovery system we eliminate receiving chips during the first year and celebrate only the 2nd conuinctio instead, which is done after the fifth step. If the sponsor doesn't believe that his charge has achieved the 2nd conuinctio, then the sponsor should discontinue sponsorship. However, if the two of them celebrate the 2nd conuinctio, then the sponsee can get the first annual chip when that time comes.

6. Were entirely ready to have the group remove all these defects of character

The time has come for the sponsee to really get down to working on himself. The rubedo is the third stage and its color is red. Red was thought by alchemists to contain the essence of life. Medieval people believed that the soul resided in the blood and the heart was therefore the spiritual and physical center of a person's life. From here on, it's all about change. The sponsee has only one thing to change, and that's every*thing*, so all the baggage he's carrying from the wreckage of the past needs to be disposed of. Homework:

Do you have any fairy tales or myths that you feel a special affinity with? Why? Describe situations and events where you have been full of pride. What has this brought into your life that you like? What problems has it caused you? Describe activities you really enjoy, except addictive behavior, of course. What are some healthy eating or exercise habits that you could start? What are some unhealthy eating habits that you could give up? Describe some secret *good* deeds that you have done or would like to do. Describe situations and events where you have been greedy, overly needy or materialistic. Describe situations where you have given in to lust without regard for others or morality. What problems has it caused you? Describe situations when you've been dishonest. What problems has it caused you? Are you ready to depend upon the group to help keep you honest? Describe situations when you've been envious or jealous of others. What problems has it caused? Are you ready to share these situations in meetings? Describe situations where you have avoided responsibility for your actions or lack of actions. What problems has it caused? Are you ready to allow the group to help you take responsibility for your actions? List your major defects of character. What do you plan to do when these major defects of character start to become evident? List each defect individually along with the proposed preventive behavior and how you'll allow the group and/or your sponsor to help you in your battle against these defects.

7. Humbly ask the group to help remove our shortcomings

Timing is an essential factor in inner alchemy. Twelve-steppers have noticed repeatedly that a member will hear something clearly only when the time is right. Sponsors may continually point out something with no results. Then the sponsee informs him that he or she has discovered a great truth that is exactly what the sponsor had been trying to get across all along. Timing is a great mystery, for it cannot be controlled by us. At a certain moment, an experience that would have been impossible a week before unfolds with no difficulty. The alchemists warned that all haste was of the devil; rushing violates the gradual evolution that accords with time. As the Chinese philosophers well knew, to be in accord with time makes the difference between success and failure. It's not conducive to our recovery to beat ourselves up when his happens, but it is conducive to our recovery to listen to what's being said in meetings and by sponsors. Homework:

What have you heard in meetings that you have actually chosen to ignore because you didn't like who was speaking? What other defects will be most difficult to give up? In what order do you plan to give them up? What kinds of situations, stressors or pressure cause you to regress back into your defects of character? What can you do to lessen the likelihood of that stress occurring? What makes you lose hope? Can you avoid such situations? If so, how? What (person, situation, event, thought) restores your hope? Describe in detail how you think your life will be different without your defects of character. What are you grateful for? (I've heard it said that grateful people are happy people). When were you the happiest? Describe your typical day's activities in terms of how much time you spend on each type of activity. Describe your typical day's activities if you knew that you had only one year to live. Have you decided how much time you spend with loved ones? What can you do to contribute to the *anima mundi* (soul of the world) - making the world a better place?

8. Made a list of all persons we had harmed and became willing to make amends to them all

Like the fourth and fifth steps, the next two action steps are imperative for an enduring peace of mind, and essential for the third conuinctio. It's very unlikely that anyone can live a happy and productive life if they're carrying around unresolved baggage. The third conuinctio is our final destination, but we have the rest of our lives to sustain it. The third conuinctio is the philosopher's stone, individuation of the recovery process - the Gold. Homework:

What important relationships did you destroy or damage because of your addiction? List all those people that you have possibly harmed by your addiction. List the effect on them and on you and on your relationship with them. Take the list of people that you have harmed, and list possible amends for each of them. What consequences do you fear in making amends? List the worst and the best things that can happen? What is likely to happen? Do you feel angry or resentful toward any people on your amends list? If so, write them a letter of anger, but don't send it. Describe any other ways that you've used to get rid of the anger and resentment toward anyone on your list. Depth psychology is the psychology of the unconscious, of which dreams are a part. Describe any dreams, if any, that relate to making amends to others.

9. Made direct amends to such people whenever possible, except when to do so would inure them or others

Once the list is made, and the essential homework in connection to the list, then the sponsee is ready to start a process that sometimes takes years. This is one of those steps that doesn't always get finished, but it's necessary to keep it in mind and apply it whenever the opportunity arises. Homework:

What amends do you think you have already made? These can include apologies already made, helpful tasks for those that you have hurt, changed attitudes and so forth. Remember, however, amends are more than just apologies, but often an apology is all you can do. From your list of amends, if there are apologies that you need to make, write them down first. Read your apologies to the group, a friend or your sponsor and ask if it sounds sincere or if it sounds defensive or like an attack on the other person. Record what response they have about them. After you've had your first encounter with making amends, record what happened. How did you feel about it? How did the other person respond? What have you learned from it? What would you do differently next time? After having done your first several amends, record your overall impressions. Is there anything common? Has anything surprised or disappointed you? Which amends have or will be the most difficult? What do you need to do to be able to make these amends? How are you dealing with being compelled to defend yourself? Again, have you had any dreams about making amends? If so, describe as much of them that you can remember. Yes, recovery is a lot of work.

10. Continued to take personal inventory and when we were wrong promptly admitted it

This is a maintenance step that will be worked periodically for the rest of the sponsee's life, providing he remains abstinent that long. We have a natural tendency to not admit when we're wrong. The philosopher's stone cannot be achieved unless we're capable of doing this - despite how embarrassing or humiliating it might be. Individuation of the recovery process is a status not all people in recovery actually achieve. How can a sponsor elevate his sponsee to the ultimate level if he is still operating on an external locus of control? The philosopher's stone - the Gold - cannot be achieved unless an internal locus of control has been mastered. If we place the blame for everything negative in our lives 'out there' and not take ownership of our part in it, then we're operating in an external locus of control. If we are truly accountable for all of our actions and are unhesitatingly willing to admit our wrongs, then we can say that we are really operating on an internal locus of control. But this is a process, we get better and better at it as time progress, providing we are actively and continually working on it. Homework:

What is your plan to allow time for reflection each day? What new behaviors would you like to try to make your alchemical journey more effective? How would you go about implementing these? What strategies do you need to stay away from the stinking thinking that so many addicts have such a hard time letting go of? What are your triggers for addictive behavior? How can you guard against them or prepare for them?

11. Sought through introspection or meditation to improve our conscious contact with humanity

If we were contumacious assholes during our addiction, then this step serves as a monitor to keep us in check so that we won't be that way anymore. Everybody needs introspection, but far from everybody participates in this spiritual notion. The world we live in can be viewed as hostile or amicable. We can't achieve the level of individuation - the Gold - we desire if we don't view our fellow men and women as partners rather than antagonists. Homework:

Can you recall a time when your life was heading in the wrong direction? If so, what brought you back? Describe this in detail. How would you describe your outlook and beliefs concerning humanity? What are your favorite sources of wisdom and knowledge about healthy values? If you were stranded on a desert island with the option of choosing one book, which book would you choose? Why? If you had only one week to live and unlimited resources, who would you gather around you and how would you pass the time? Write a full page of what

73

you would like your obituary to say.

12. Having had a spiritual awakening as the result of these steps, we tried to carry this message to addicts, and to practice these principles in all our affairs

If a sponsee is uncertain what a spiritual awakening/experience is, like I was for ten years into my recovery, then he or she can read my research on spiritual experience in my book *Scumbag Sewer Rats: An Archetypal Understanding of Criminalized Drug Addicts*. This is original research where I interviewed and tape-recorded addicts and alcoholics, asking that they tell me about their spiritual experiences. Homework:

Have you been able to reach out to another recovering addict? If so, describe the situation and how it feels to you. What do you say if someone asks how the recovery process has worked for you? How do you usually handle conflict? Do you know of any way to be more effective in conflict resolution? If so, how would you become more effective? How much time are you willing to devote to working with others on their program? What outside resources can you call on when you need help as a sponsor? Do you want to be a sponsor? List the reasons why or why not.

Once the third conuinctio has occurred, which can be from six months to several years, the addict has achieved individuation of the recovery process. The content of the alchemical vessel has turned into Gold. He has become the philosopher's stone. He has recovered from a seemingly hopeless case of mind and body. Again, the alchemical imagery and processes will continue to be used, and hopefully the sponsee will also have found a life worth living and an enduring interest in the spiritual aspects of recovery and of alchemical transformation and alchemy in general.

Archetypes & Culture
The wounded healer is an archetypal dynamic that may be constellated in an analytic relationship. Whereas sponsors don't practice psychoanalysis without a license like they do in the psychotherapeutic relationship of sponsor and sponsee, what we sometimes have in

common, however, is a relationship with those we sponsor that lasts for years and sometimes the duration of our lives. The term *wounded healer* derives from the legend of Asclepius, a Greek doctor who in recognition of his own wounds established a sanctuary at Epidaurus where others could be healed of their wounds. The wounded healers in the 12-step environment are sponsors, and sponsors are addicts, and addicts personify two archetypes - the *puer aeternus* and the trickster.

Enough in this book so far has been examined concerning the *puer*. The trickster archetype, however, is more glaring because tricksters are constantly on the con, and their behaviors are wide and varied. A good example is the addict who steals his friend's dope, then helps him look for it. Here's an allegory from Cliff Walker of the wily trickster - the coyote:

> In the old days sheep farmers tried to get rid of wolves and coyotes by putting out animal carcasses laced with strychnine. The wolves, they say, were killed in great numbers, but the coyotes wised up and avoided these traps. Another story has it that when trappers set metal leg traps they will catch muskrat and mink and fox and skunk, but the coyote only rarely. Coyotes develop their own relationship to the trap; as one naturalist has written, "it is difficult to escape the conclusion that coyotes . . . have a sense of humor. How else to explain, for instance, the well-known propensity of experienced coyotes to dig up traps, turn them over, and urinate or defecate on

Addicts are tricky, but most of them are intelligent, and that combination makes addiction very difficult to overcome. That's why recovery is so much work.

Puer and trickster psychology of the chemically dependent is a cultural phenomenon. From the time I started using drugs, it didn't matter where I went, I could usually identify people of my own ilk. Going to jail wasn't much of a threat because my type of people was there.

The cultural ethos of 12-step programs is similar. We can go to a meeting and get help from people just like us. Those who adapt to the 12-step environment often recover. Hopefully we can put a dent in the amount of people who give up, or don't try 12-step programs in the first place, because of their discomfort with all the God talk - which is the reason I've developed the alchemical approach to recovery borrowing from the twelve steps. When I first wrote this paper, I was fascinated with alchemy and 12-step programs, and I believed this alternative method is an effective option for those who are interested. This paper has been expanded and revised into a full-length book which will be published in 2015, but the expanded version doesn't borrow as much from the 12 steps as this paper does.

Chapter Six References

Raff, Jeffrey. (2000). *Jung and the alchemical imagination*. York Beach, Maine: Nicolas-Hays, Inc.

Schwartz-Salant, Nathan. (1995). *Jung on alchemy*. Princeton, NJ: Princeton University Press.

Walker, Clifford. (1999). *One eye closed the other red: The california bootlegging years*. Barstow, CA: Back Door Publishing.

CHAPTER SEVEN

Prison Recidivism

> The roots of the word prison come from prisune from
> before 1112, which means confinement. Prisune was
> influenced by pris, which means taken or seized. From
> Latin prehenso - to lay hold of, clutch at. Prysner - one
> kept in prison: probably 1350-75.

Is prison a deterrent to crime? Judging by the recidivism rate, no. Many see recidivism as the result of a perversion of the formal aims of imprisonment. What are the formal aims of imprisonment? Foucault (1977) says that formal punishment started as revenge, then shifted to the defense of society (p. 90). We could easily say that it has shifted back to revenge when considering such statements as "lock him up and throw the key away," or "he got exactly what he deserved."

Many People probably have a difficult time admitting that their idea of punishment is really revenge. However, the ones who opt for the defense-of-society approach to punishment, should probably consider what is going on behind the walls of our prisons, specifically in the federal prison system and the California Department of Corrections. Those who want revenge certainly would not want to continue to pay an astronomical amount of tax dollars to make sure the inhabitants of such a den of hedonists are so well taken care of, some might even say - pampered - not to mention the money interminably spent building prisons.

Walking onto a prison yard for the first time can often ease the tension of a first offender. He will see inmates playing handball, basketball, and some throwing Frisbees. Others are working out on a weight pile, and still others playing cards on picnic tables. On the other side of the yard a softball game might even be going on, with all the and cheers characteristically heard in a baseball stadium. "Hey, this might not be too bad!"

Prior to emphasizing the benefits of a federal correctional institution in Pennsylvania, Worth (1995) explains that "with visitors, it's like a joke, to see how long before they compare this place to a college campus." Federal prisons have had the reputation as "resorts" or "country clubs" for a long time.

Besides being well cared for, their fellow inmates are educating them in ways that increase recidivism. There is not much doubt that prison conforms to the old-fashioned image of a "school of crime." Therefore, many commit crimes with impunity. Correctional institutions create, maintain, and reinforce criminal patterns of behavior by housing first-time offenders and veterans together. The mixing of petty offenders with serious and dangerous ones is counterproductive. The only ones that are consistently segregated are the sex offenders - mostly pedophiles.

Smolowe (1994) shares that;

> Americans' impatience for quick-fix remedies resembles the frustration that drives inner-city youths to seize on illegal get-rich schemes: they want to cut corners, produce high yields and not pay a price. But grim experience indicates that, as with crime, hard time does not always pay the anticipated dividends. When money is poured into building another prison at the expense of rebuilding a prisoner's self-image, it is often just a prelude to more - and worse - crime. They start as drug offenders, they eventually become property-crime offenders, and then they commit crimes against people. They learn this trade as they go through the prison system.

There are multiple, repeat offenders that find prison life more appealing than life on the outside because prison reinforces their sense of irresponsibility: they don't have to pay rent or utility bills, they don't have to work (though most do in leu of being isolated), they don't have anything to worry about relating to real life responsibilities, except when their next visit is arriving, or who they are going to con to keep a steady influx of amenities or drugs.

The Latin term *puer aeternus* translates to eternal boy (or lad) in

English. Marie-Louse von Franz (2000) describes the *puer* as one who "remains too long in adolescent psychology; that is, all those characteristics that are normal in a youth of seventeen or eighteen are continued into later life." (p. 7). Characteristic of the *puer* is a gross lack of responsibility. "The one thing," stresses von Franz, "he absolutely refuses his responsibility for anything, or to carry the weight of a situation." (p. 9).

Kiley (1983) offers another interpretation of the *puer aeternus* as the victim of the peter pan syndrome. He shares that "they can't escape irresponsibility. This trap begins as innocent, typical rebellion, but mushrooms into an adult lifestyle." (p. 45). The prisons are full of people with rebellious lifestyles.

Many of these people have reputations as fabulists, card-carrying storytellers, also known in medical circles as confabulators. Most of them are jailhouse lawyers. They tell their loved ones that their excuses are reasons; they will break promises with impunity, then seriously wonder why people get angry with them for it. Most of them believe that everybody behaves as they do, and this behavior is characteristic of irresponsible, rebellious and self-serving lifestyles.

Most parolees will say that they don't want to return to prison; but unconsciously their behavior is saying, "catch me, so I can go back home and be with my friends where I'll be taken care of and provided for." How is a person in prison prepared to live a law-abiding life on the outside? For the most part, they aren't. Prison relieves him of responsibility. Glasser (1965) writes that "he broke the law not because he was angry or bored, but because he was irresponsible." (p. 15).

Once on the yard, even a first offender is going to seek out his own kind, and there are all kinds on the yard. They come from all walks of life, and they make friends easily, especially if they are repeat offenders - they are the old-home-week types that cope easily because their kind of people are right there with them. Dealing with this is much more difficult because the more they return to prison, the more friends they accumulate. Prison loses its deterrent impact once a person has been through it. They learn that they can survive in or out and they do not fear going to prison anymore. So, restorative justice (if there is or was ever such a thing) is a one-shot deal, otherwise etiolation is likely.

For the institutionalized men in prison, women are viewed as potential conquests, sexual receptacles and suppliers of goods and services. That is why visiting day, for many prisoners, is often more of an obligation than a joy, except, of course, when the visit is conjugal. The visiting room on a Saturday looks like an overeaters anonymous meeting. Inmates often seek obesely, less attractive women because they are more susceptible to the flowery words that flow from their correspondence. These women are more likely to be lonely and have low self-esteem, which is easily capitalized on by players in the joint. To the inmate, a woman is little more than a business proposition, of use only so long as she is profitable. Time spent on her is an investment that is expected to pay off and usually does.

In *The Oxford History of the Prison*, Morris (1995) offers "One Day in the Life of #12345."

> If you expect the usual prison tale of constant violence, brutal guards, gang rapes, daily escape efforts, turmoil, and fearsome adventures, you will be deeply disappointed. Prison life is really nothing like what the press, television, and movies suggest. It is not a daily round of threats, fights, plots, and 'shanks' (prison-made knives). (p. 203).

Being released from prison can be frightening because being responsible and accountable for their existence is alien to them. Prison has either enervated them or rendered them lackadaisical. Here is an excerpt from the Chaplain's Report (1948) from Alcatraz: "Escape is the same dangerous phenomenon whether it takes place in the overt violence of a prison break or in the subtle escape of psychological irresponsibility."

For inmates approaching release, the fears of life outside the prison walls seem to counteract the frustrations and hardships they experienced inside. Many start remembering that freedom is not all that it's cracked up to be. Soon they come to realize that they are living more comfortably inside than many are on the outside. Prison begins looking more like a refuge, like the archetypal mother who provides and protects. However, concerning mothers, Jung (1970) shares that "the mythological Great Mothers are usually a danger to their sons. Jeremias mentions a fish representation on an early Christian lamp, showing one fish devouring the other." (CW 9ii. Par 174). The penitentiary is obviously a danger to its sons, devouring them in such a way as to keep them continually coming back. In *A Dictionary of Symbols,* Cirlot (1971) says "for Jung, the Magna Mater represents the objective truth of Nature, masquerading, or incarnate, in the figure of a maternal woman, a sybil, a goddess or a priestess, but sometimes taking the form of a church, for instance, or a city or district." (p. 132). Or, in this case - a prison.

Those who are under the impression that prison is a lonely place, consider the fact that prisoners are never really alone. In minimum security prisons, they house inmates in dorms of various capacities. In the higher security institutions, they house the population in multiple-man cells and there are usually at least two people to a cell. Even on blocks with single cells there is someone in the cell next door, across the way, or down the tier. This is even true in the hole and in control units, where verbal and nonverbal communication flows no matter how hard the guards try to stop it. Since they rarely get to be alone while serving time, being alone after being released (which happens often), suddenly makes them dispirited, uncomfortable or even afraid.

Morris & Rothman (1995) describes a survey carried out by the National Council on Crime and Delinquency where the situation of American penal institutions was characterized:

> Offenders in such institutions are not as likely to commit further crimes while serving their sentences, but the conditions in which they live are the poorest possible preparation for their successful reentry into society, and often merely reinforces in them a pattern of manipulation or destructiveness. (p. 173).

We all have comfort zones. Many alcoholics think of bars and taverns as their homes away from home. The comfort zone for a gambler is a casino or the race track. Returning to the old haunts feels comfortable. Familiarity is the hallmark of comfort zones. Leder (2000) quotes John as saying that "once we get out of that lifestyle we don't know what to

81

do." (p. 191). Leader continues:

> you were the Man - now you feel like a lost boy. And the day looms empty, without sensation or purpose. How can this inner void resist the gathering forces of the same old street, the same old dealers, the offer of a free blow? (p. 191).

Like the victory gained over the Romans at Heracles' Asculum in 279 B.C. by Pyrrhus, the ones who succeed and prosper after serving long prison terms have achieved a pyrrhic victory over the odds against them.

There are many success stories of pyrrhic victories over obstacles of all kinds. It would be a pyrrhic victory, indeed, if we could really rehabilitate our country's prison population, or better yet, find a way to keep them from going there in the first place. I think Jung would agree that prison, like churches and cities, is playing the role of the great mother. We don't have a chance at combating recidivism until the populace realizes that the system we've been using for so long doesn't work. Part of society wants punishment and another part wants prison reform. Prison reform reinforces recidivism and so does punishment. Either way, it is a self-perpetuating system. I am reminded of how 12-step meetings end, with the joining of hands and the words spoken in unison: "Keep coming back, it works!" Prison guards should do the same thing.

Chapter Seven References

Cirlot, J.E. (1995). *A dictionary of symbols*. New York: Barnes & Noble.

Foucault, Michel. (1991). *Discipline & punish: the birth of the prison*. New York: Vantage Books.

Fromm, Erich. (1961). *Escape from freedom*. New York: Holt, Rinehard and Winston.

Glasser, William. (1975). *Reality therapy: A new approach to psychiatry*. New York: Harper & Row Publishers.

Jung, Carl. (1970). *Aion*. Princeton, N.J.: Princeton University Press.

Kiley, Dan. (1983). *The peter pan syndrome: men who have never grown up.* New York: Dodd, Mead & Co.

Leder, Drew. (2000). *The soul knows no bars: Inmates reflect on life, death, & hope.* New York: Rowman & Littlefield Publishers, Inc.

Morris, Norval, & Rothman, David J. (Eds.). (1998). *The oxford history of the prison: The practice of punishment in western society*. New York: Oxford University Press.

Smethers, John. (1995). "Prison–the day care center." *Pleiades Magazine*, Vol 11, No. 9.

Smolowe, Jill. (Feb 7, 1994). "And throw away the key." *Time*: Domestic, Vol 143, No. 6 [On-line], at www.time.com/time/magazine/archive/1994/940207/940207.cover.priso ns.htm.

von Franz, Marie-Louise. (2000). *The problem of the puer aeternus*. Toronto, Canada: Inner City Books.

Worth, Robert. (November, 1995). "A model prison." *The Atlantic Monthly* [On-line], at www.theatlantic.com/issues/95nov/prisons/prisons.htm.

CHAPTER EIGHT

A Parable to the Mythological Gilgamesh

To decide during childhood, whether as an ideal from a dream or fantasy, or from being impressed or influenced by others in the community, to delve into the netherworld of drugs and alcohol - actually choosing to live a life of chaos - is one of those mysteries of human behavior. Most addicts do not wake up one morning and say, "Gee, I think I'll spend my life as a drug addict." Perhaps not quite that literally, but many of us do make such decisions, usually unconsciously, however. Leonard (I 989) shares that "all addictions are killers; each in its own way kills living in the moment, kills creativity, love, and the trusting faith of the inner child. Archetypally, The Killer is the inner character who decides against life (p. 196). Little do we know, those of us who take that route do not realize that "no one ascends from the underworld unmarked" (Inanna,p. 68). We are often warned, however:

> Gilgamesh, you are young, your courage carries you too far, you cannot know what this enterprise means which you plan. We have heard that Humbaba is not like men who die, his weapons are such that none can stand against them; the forest stretched for ten thousand leagues in every direction; who would willingly go down to explore its depths? As for Humbaba, when he roars it is like the torrent of the storm, his breath is like fire and his jaws are death itself. Why do you crave to do this thing, Gilgamesh? It is no equal struggle when one fights with Humbaba, that battering-ram. (Gilgamesh, p. 73-74)

"Little boy, you are young, your courage carries you too far, you cannot know what this enterprise means which you plan." Unfortunately, there are usually no counselors of Uruk who can warn the contemporary little Gilgamesh. Typically, around junior high school age, little Gilgamesh starts drinking on the weekends and is inevitably offered a few hits of a joint, a line of crank or coke, or some pharmaceutical substance or black-market equivalent, which is the prelude to a life in the abyss. His delusional, self-proclaimed omniscience will gradually descend him and his cohorts into the company of the Erinyes. But first, as his initiatory prelude to the nekyia (also called first-stage alcoholism/addiction), he must do battle with Humbaba.

"I have a long journey to go, to the Land of Humbaba, I must travel an unknown road and fight a strange battle" (Gilgamesh, p. 74). In the world of addiction, Humbaba is an invisible foe, and his weapons are alluring. Little Gilgamesh will smoke that joint to impress Alice - Alice, who is already in wonderland, lures him with her charms - "c'mon little boy, let's go to my place." Then, after having developed a penchant for stealing, being expelled from school, jailed, and kicked out of his parents' home, little Gilgamesh will sell drugs - the money he can use for flashy cars, nice clothes, and an infamous reputation that will make other little Gilgameshes want to follow his ignominious lead. These are Humbaba's weapons. "Humbaba, when he roars it is like the torrent of the storm, his breath is like fire and his jaws are death itself. Why do you crave to do this thing, Gilgamesh?" Gilgamesh does not heed these fatidic projections. Unconsciously, he wants to lose the battle so he can start his descent to the flashy, exciting fires of the Inferno.

In Uruk he abandoned his [home] to descend to the Underworld.

In Badtibra he abandoned his [school] to descend to the Underworld.

In Zabalam he abandoned his [family] to descend to the Underworld.

In Adab he abandoned his [morals] to descend to the Underworld.

In Nippur he abandoned his [health] to descend to the Underworld.

In Kish he abandoned his [dreams] to descend to the Underworld

In Akkad he abandoned his [soul] to descend to the Underworld. (Inanna, p. 520)

Enkidu - faithful companion, before your descent, please tell little Gilgamesh that a farrago of difficulties awaits him; tell little Gilgamesh that county jail or prison awaits him; tell him that hepatitis and cirrhosis awaits him; tell him that unhappiness and guilt awaits him; tell him that mental institutions and the morgue awaits him; and tell little Gilgamesh that Anhanga' awaits him.

Anhanga is the devil of the Amazon Indians of Brazil. According to the myth,

> Anhanga is a formless shape-shifter who can assume many identities. He is a prankster who delights in tricking humans. The dark god is also adept at filling people's minds with horrific visions of the supernatural, including frightening images of a horrific afterlife (Encyclopedia of Hell).

The Descent

To no avail - Gilgamesh is not afraid. Addicts are not afraid. It doesn't matter what happens to them, they will predictably go back for more, for they are *non compos mentis* - not of a sound mind. They will get out of prison, then repeat the refractory behavior and expect different results. They will get out of the hospital and continue the scabrous practices that got them there in the first place. They will get DUI's, then get behind the wheel, and decide that *nunces bibendum* - now it is time to drink. They will make solemn promises, then break them. While immured in the Underworld, they will continually hurt the ones they love, not unlike how Inanna hurt her loved ones. Wolkstein (I 983) explains that;

> Meanwhile, Inanna's servant and two sons, who care deeply about her, have abandoned the routine of their daily lives. Ninshubur waits by the gate of the underworld for Inanna. Shara and Lulal, Inanna's sons, wait for their mother in their temples, most likely praying. All three have taken off their customary clothes and put on sackcloth, the garment of mourning. (p. 161)

The poem version renders a more graphic depiction:

> When, after three days and three nights, Inanna had not returned, Ninshubur set up a lament for her by the ruins.
>
> She beat the drum for her in the assembly places.
>
> She circled the houses of gods.
>
> She tore at her eyes; she tore at her mouth; she tore at her thighs. (Inanna, p. 61)

Gilgamesh' descent into the Underworld keeps his friends and family continually worrying about him. Mothers and wives of addicts like Gilgamesh, alone in their desperation, will tear at themselves in worry. When the addict is around friends and family, he or she will lie, steal, and manipulate them. Gilgamesh, for example, is sitting on the sofa at a friend's house. In walks his friend and asks "hey bro, have you seen my stash (drugs)." Gilgamesh retorts "what are ya askin *me* for, I didn't take it!" Then after a little more discussion, Gilgamesh starts helping his fiend tear the house apart looking for the stash. That is the turpitude of an addict - he'll steal your dope, and then help you look for it! That is the way of the Underworld. "The ways of the underworld are perfect. They may not be questioned" (Innana, p. 58). An addict interacts with others by manipulating and using them to fulfill addictive needs. Doing this takes a certain amount of self- confidence: an ability to assert oneself, or an ability to appear helpless to get others to act as caretakers.

Blandae mendacia Linguae - lies of a smooth tongue, and other dark practices by Gilgamesh are conpounded by additional complexities concerning family members. Family members can't bring themselves to believe that their son/daughter, brother/sister would stoop so low. Eventually, however, they cannot deny it any longer and they get angry. Wolkstein (1983), offers an analogy: She shares that

> Entil, Inanna's father's father, the authority and director of the rational world, wants nothing to do with Inanna in the kur. Nanna, Inanna's father and good son of Enlil, also has no appreciation or understanding of why Inanna might have gone on such a journey. Both Enlil and Nanna are angry that Inanna should pursue a direction that is different from theirs. (p. 159)

Often both husband and wife are addicts, and each of them behave, scandalously, like *anguis in herba* - snakes in the grass. In addition to tumultuous assaults and casting aspersions on one another, for pecuniary purposes they will steal from one another to keep from going to jail. They will tell on one another, and for a bag of dope they will be unfaithful to one another. A good example is the following joke:

Two couples were playing cards one evening. Gilgamesh dropped a card on the floor. When he bent down to pick it up, he noticed that

Enkidu's wife's legs were spread wide, and she was not wearing panties! Shocked by this, Gilgamesh hit his head on the table and emerged red-faced. Later, Gilgamesh went to the kitchen to get a beer. Enkidu's wife followed and asked "Did you see something you liked under the card table?" Surprised by her boldness, Gilgamesh admitted that he did. She said, "well, you can have it for $500." After thinking about it for about a millisecond, Gilgamesh agrees. She tells him to be at her house around 2pm Friday. Gilgamesh shows up at Enkidu's house at 2pm sharp, and after paying her the $500., they did their thing. Afterward, Gilgamesh left. As usual, Enkidu came home from work at 6pm and upon entering the house asks his wife "Honey, did Gilgamesh come by the house this afternoon?" With a lump in her throat, she answered, "Why yes, he did." Her heart nearly skipped a beat when Enkidu asked, "and did he give you $500?" After mustering up her best poker face, she replied, "well, yes, in fact he did." Enkidu, with a satisfied look on his face, said "good, I was hoping he did. Gilgamesh came by the office this morning and borrowed $500 from me. He promised that he would stop by here on his way home to pay me back. This nefarious parable is classic drug addict behavior, admirably earning the archetypal descriptor of trickster.

Though not a drug addict, Inanna was a woman scorned by her husband:

> I placed him on the throne, gave him his position. I loved him and he left me to attend to affairs of state. While I went to deal with matters affecting my deepest soul, he used my powers to make himself more important. Once I was his whole world - now he refuses to descend from his throne to help me. (Inanna, p. 162)

In true drug-addict fashion, she retaliates and sacrifices him. How many other family members will suffer other kinds of hell during little Gilgamesh's descent (also referred to as second stage alcoholism/addiction)?

The time comes when his friends will abandon him, but family members are often taken hostage, much like Persephone was taken hostage by Hades. Whereas Persephone was taken hostage into the

Underworld of Hades, Gilgamesh's family members are also taken hostage into the Underworld - into the Underworld of psychological illness. Families of addicts most always become as dysfunctional as their addicted relatve.

I have opted not to include parables or information on third-stage alcoholism/addiction in the interest of brevity. Most people do not ascend (recover) from the third stage anyway.

According to Miller and Gorski (1982),

> When family life becomes painful, chaotic, and unpredictable because of addictive behavior, the family reorganizes itself around new roles, new rules, and new rituals that protect it from disintegration. As resentments develop in the family, productive communication may cease to exist. Family members withdraw from one another because of the pain of interaction, and they withdraw from people outside the family because of the fear of exposure. There is no consistency or dependability in any area of family life (p. 28).

Gilgamesh needs treatment. His family needs treatment. With treatment, a return - or an ascent (typically called recovery) back to the day world can occur.

The Ascent

The entire family can seek therapy with family therapists. They can also attend Al-Anon or Nar-Anon meetings, which don't cost anything. At no cost Gilgamesh can attend 12-step meetings, and there are various other forms of treatment available for him in recovery homes/treatment centers. Concentrating on the plight of the addicts recovery, Leonard (1989) reminds us that

> Dionysus was connected with addiction, as the god of wine and revelry, and with creativity, as the god of drama. The addict, like Dionysus, is dismembered, torn into pieces, through the addictive process. But as Dionysus is reborn in a new cycle of creation, so is the addict in recovery (p. 81).

Recovery can also be thought of as an alchemical process. The first coniunctio (conjunction) is the transformation from the dregs of active addiction to the clamor of abstinence. There is a death - the death of an inveterate lifestyle. Raff (2000) says that;

> The ego that has reached this level in the work and will have the nasty surprise of meeting its own death. If it is fluid and open enough to allow that experience to occur unhindered, it will quickly move to the next stage (p. 118).

Of course, Gilgamesh may not allow that experience to occur unhindered; therefore, the clamor of abstinence often results in a relapse. The second coniunctio is the transformation from abstinence to recovery. There is a death: the death of the dragon's teeth (seeds of strife) for recovery. According to Raff (2000),

> Dorn called the second coniunctio the bodily union, and this reference is very significant. To move from the mental union to the bodily union indicates that integration has occurred; that is, what had previously been only an idea has become a living reality (p. 133).

During the stage of abstinence, Gilgamesh is literally trudging the road to happy destiny. Once the second coniunctio occurs, what was for varying periods of time only an idea becomes a living reality. The third coniunctio I don't include as part of the recovery process. Since the emotional development of an addict is callow, it stops at the onset of the addictive process. The alchemical process of recovery can only hope to attain enough maturity to start the process again in order to individuate. However, the second coniunctio is a mental and emotional halcyon compared with the imbroglio of active addiction. We can finally see *lux mundi* or varnah - the light of glory.

The ways of the underworld may be perfect, but we often do not agree with them. If one is fortunate enough to ascend, there will have been a price to pay. Wolkstein (1983) offers a parabola:

> After losing her bridegroom through her uncontrollable willfulness, Inanna realizes she has lost the "sweetness" of life.

In "The Huluppu-Tree," the young Inanna wept because she could not get her way. In "Inanna and the God of Wisdom" and "The Courtship," she was able to channel her resources to achieve her desires. But now, having returned from the underworld charged with her own dark, ruthless powers, the widowed Inanna grieves because she has pushed her way through and destroyed the bridegroom and husband she loves. (Inanna, p. 165)

The wreckage of the past can be an enduring nuisance: prison record, health problems, estranged families, debts, and learning how to live all over again are just a few examples. Most aggravating to many people in recovery trying to forge a new life in a society that's often unforgiving, is like trying to swim in the river of forgetfulness. "Unfortunately," writes Hillman (1979),

> Psychology emphasizes attention and recall; the dayworld wishes to have, must absolutely have, a 'good memory'; a bad memory is more devastating to success than is a bad conscience. Forgetting therefore becomes a pathological sign. But depth psychology based on an archetypal perspective might understand forgetting as serving a deeper purpose, seeing in these holes and slips in the dayworld the means by which events are transformed out of personal life, voiding it, emptying it. Somehow we must come to better terms with Lethe [river of forgetfulness], since she rules many years, especially the last years, and we would be foolish to dismiss her work only as pathological. (p. 154)

"Especially the last years," Hillman said. Well, we can add the chthonic years of addiction too. What deeper purpose could Lethe be serving to a recovering addict? Maybe the river of forgetfulness will serve as an ancilla. If Gilgamesh, for example, could remember everything he did during those years, self-forgiveness may not be possible. Hillman (1979) suggests that;

> ..what is being forgotten out of the dayworld of our lives may be making possible the inflow of another sort of remembrance by turning our attention from chasing the lost bit of data to the

empty, sinking feeling that forgetting leaves behind. (p. 154)

If re-membering the past of Gilgamesh's addiction is supplanted with another sort of re-membrance, such as how much he admired his high school social studies teacher, then maybe he can re-member the education ethic his parents instilled in him. The nexus between his teacher and his father might render Gilgamesh susceptible to an education.

Obviously, there is more to recovery than dealing with a *lapsus memoriae* - a slip of the memory, but it is a start. Between the various forms of treatment available, and a remembering of the past, Gilgamesh can lead a four square and happy life, just as the union of Inanna and Dumuzi represents the reawakening of life in the spring.

Conclusion
Parts of the hypothetical Gilgamesh above were my own experience, and some was the plight of addicts in general. Having spent more than 30 years in hedone, I consider myself lucky to have emerged as an incipient opsimath and found my way to higher education. Who knows, maybe it was because of Hillman's suggestion about "making possible the inflow of another sort of remembrance." Ending up *intra muros*, within the walls of the California Department of Corrections is often thought of as a bottom. Bottoms are often good things. If I had not been lucky enough to get into the prison system and a subsequent substance abuse education program while I was incarcerated, I would have certainly returned to my previous cipherous lifestyle upon release, which is what most addicts do - *mea culpa*.

Chapter Eight References

Hillman, J. (I 979). *The dream and the underworld*. New York: Harper & Row Publishers.
Jung, C. (I 953). *Psychology and alchemy*. New York: Pantheon Books. Leonard, L. (I 9 89). Witness to the fire: Creativity and the veil of addiction. Boston, Massachusetts: Shambhala Publications, Inc.

Miller, M. & Gorski, T. (1982). *Family recovery: Growing beyond addiction*. Independence, Missouri: Independence Press.

Raff, J. (2000). *Jung and the alchemical imagination*. New York: Nicolas-Hays, Inc.

The Epic of Gilgamesh. (N. K. Sanders, Trans.). (1972). New York: Penguin Books. (Original work 2000 B.C.E.).

Van Scott, M. (Ed.). (1998). *Encyclopedia of hell* (1st ed.). New York: St. Martin's Press.

Wolkstein, D. & Kramer, S. (Eds.). *Inanna: Queen of heaven and earth: Her stories and hymns from sumer*. (Original work 2000 B.C.E.). New York: Harper & Row Publishers.

CHAPTER NINE

Causes and Conditions

Part I

A ddictive behavior in parents often begets addictive behavior in their offspring. According to Nakken (1988),

> If a child grows up in a family in which one parent is an addict, the child is likely to develop an addiction. If both parents are addicts, the child's chances of addiction increases. Subsequently, the generational cycle of addiction continues. When adult children of addicts seek relationships, it is usually with people who are similar. This search doesn't happen on a conscious level.

As mentioned in a previous paper, teenagers usually live for the moment. So do practicing addicts. Emotionally, addicts act and think like teenagers. Many issues that addicts struggle with are very similar to what teenagers struggle with. The difference is that addicts stay trapped in the mind-set of a teenager as long as they're living a life centered around drugs and/or alcohol.

It has been suggested that the tendency toward addiction is biological, inherited genetically, or a result of chemical imbalances. Cohen (1988) notes that;

> It is easy to postulate that the reinforcement centers in the ventral teg mentum, the locus ceruleus, the mediolateral frontal cortex, or the nucleus accumbens have an inborn deficiency of catecholamines or that the receptors are hyposensitive. Alternatively, perhaps the endogenous opioids are congenitally in short supply, or the delta opioid receptor is deficient in quantity or quality. Will diagnoses like 'hypoendorphism' or 'opioid receptor insufficiency' or 'hypodopaminosis' ever be made with reliability?

Probably not.

Research reported by Kinney and Leaton (1995) suggest that heredity isn't as simple as what was previously believed.

> At conception, we receive a unique set of genetic material - internal instructions that guide growth and development. These instructions set limits in the form of predispositions. The outcome will depend on unique life circumstances and environment. Some people remain thin without effort and others put on weight easily. This example of a genetic predisposition for weight correlates with a genetic predisposition for addiction. Combined with life circumstances, addictive behavior is likely. To complicate matters, the media among other causal factors, contributes its share of influence.

No one escapes the media's power to promote excess. Big businesses sell both gluttony and dieting, smoking, eroticism and an exaggerated need for the work ethic. Television commercials convey messages to addict its audience. The commercial of a lady who puts her hand to her pain-wrinkled forehead and complains "Oh, this terrible headache," is generally seen in the next scene chipper and happy, thanking a miraculous wonder drug. In the past, billboards with the Marlboro Man or Joe Camel did their part in influencing us. Other influential media, directed at youth, is the glamorization of reckless lifestyles in movies. Kids grow up in a sea of advertising. Pubescence' start seeing and hearing beer and wine ads and commercials exhorting them to drink before they are old enough. It can hardly be denied that the overall effect of advertising is to glamorize whatever it is being sold, whether it's cigarettes, alcohol or over- the-counter medication, and to encourage the idea that what is being advertised will make them feel better or enhance their lives in some way.

It appears that life events may be mediating factors in the development of psychological illness in general, and drug abuse in particular. What if a father's brother died? What if a father lost his job? What if a father had to serve a jail sentence? What if a mother was an only child - not having the large family experience, then grew up and had five children? What if she was a full-time housewife, belonged to the PTA, held a part-time job, and expected to participate in civic activities? Could addictive behavior be a coping mechanism for life events such as father's and stress such as mother's? In Bratter and Forrest, Litz (1979) reported that;

> Within a group of alcoholic and nonalcoholic women, the alcoholic group reported the impact of stress to a higher level than the nonalcoholic group. These results can apply to pre alcoholic men and women also, creating a need to relieve stress. "It calms me down, helps my nerves. It helps me unwind after a hard day.

"This explanation," says Kenny and Leaton (1995),

> ..can be viewed as the anxiety thesis. Partially a derivative of Freud's work, he stated that during times of anxiety and stress, people look to the past for things that worked for them. Theoretically, he proposed, the security of mom's breast as an infant can later influence the use of the mouth for eating, smoking and drinking disorders.

During puberty and early adolescence there is a need for identity. Young people want to break from their parents. They fall into close associations with peers, and those peers have a profound influence. Peer pressure can also come from the workplace. Bratter and Forrest state that;

> Adolescent and occupational research both suggest that drinking is a learned behavior, and that it is learned from those who have the most social influence. To be included in certain subcultures, it is necessary to drink or use drugs. Those who later develop drinking problems are likely to have started using alcohol at an earlier age than is typical for the general population. Along the same lines, the presence of a heavy-drinking partner has been found to increase both the amount and rate at which alcohol is consumed. Similar results in the number and rate of cigarettes smoked have been obtained from smokers exposed to a high-rate smoking friend as opposed to a low-rate smoking friend.

Many members of Alcoholics Anonymous claim that influences are only suggestive, that they voluntarily picked up the bottle. Nobody twisted their arm and made them drink it. It is their contention that they alone are responsible for their actions. Suggested causes, to them, are excuses that gave them permission to drink. In one of the stories in back of the Big Book of Alcoholics Anonymous (1991), a woman states that "the mental twists that led up to my drinking began many years before I ever took a drink, for I am one of those whose history proves conclusively that my drinking was a symptom of a deeper trouble."

Part II

This part of the paper has been imported from chapter one and can be skipped (to the next chapter) if the reader isn't inclined to read it again.

It is widely accepted that people use only a small percentage of their brain; therefore, little is known about what can influence parts of the brain that remains uncharted. The causes of addictive behavior discussed in Part I are also generally accepted. However, it is likely that there are more causes that we are not yet aware of. Causes from a Depth Psychological perspective should also be considered. Discussed in Part II is the addiction to perfection, obsession, fear, rebellion, oracular guidance, the collective unconscious, principles of reality and pleasure, and the shadow.

Woodman (1982) is convinced that;

The same problem is at the root of all addictions. The problem being different in each individual. The problem, whatever that may be, presents itself differently in different people. Overeating, alcoholism, gambling, sex, drug addiction, etc., are all likely symptoms of an underlying cause. Some of these causes may never be known. Others should be further investigated.

Many of us, regardless of gender, are addicted because we have been driven to specialization and perfection by our patriarchal culture. Obsession is at the root of perfection. An obsession is a persistent or recurrent idea, usually strongly tinged with emotion, and frequently involving an urge toward some kind of action, the whole mental situation being pathological. The roots of fear can also be pathological.

Without going into the many causes of fear, it must be considered a legitimate reason to lean on something for emotional support. If not properly bonded, for example, fear will most likely manifest in some way. This fear being unconscious, there is not a way to intervene. "The mother," says Woodman "who is in this situation herself because of her own heritage, cannot give her baby the strong bonding to the earth that the mother grounded in her own instincts can." Fear is often anger in disguise, and anger often produces rebellious behavior.

Rebellion encompasses various types of behavior, which include criminality and addiction. Substance abusers are characteristically thought of as rebellious. What causes rebellion? A patriarchal society can cause rebellious behavior in women. Authority figures often create rebellious behavior in both men and women. In contrast, recovery can be viewed as a form of rebellion against addiction. Therefore, rebellion doesn't have to be negative. Rebellion can result in healing. This form of rebellion is spiritual, and spirituality is an entity that should be developed.

Part of a letter published in *Pass It On* (1984) from Bill Wilson, cofounder of Alcoholics Anonymous, to Carl Jung went on to tell Jung how the message reached Bill at the low point of his own alcoholism; it described his own spiritual awakening, the subsequent founding of A.A., and the spiritual experiences of its many thousands of members. As Bill put it: "This concept proved to be the foundation of such success as Alcoholics Anonymous has since achieved. This has made conversion experience . . . available on an almost wholesale basis."

Spiritual experiences can be life changing and Dr. Jung's contribution has since changed the lives of thousands of people. Oracular guidance is also a spiritual experience. Oracular consciousness has to be developed over time; therefore, if enough time isn't devoted in developing it, what may be interpreted as oracular guidance may in reality be some other unknown influence.

98

"Give me a sign, God!" How often have people, in one way or another, sought guidance this way? But what if one does not believe that God exists? The trigger for addictive behavior is often pulled by stress or life events resulting in looking to the divine for guidance. This trigger might also be pulled by seeking oracular guidance. "To receive an oracle is to receive guidance, knowledge, or illumination from a mysterious source beyond the personal self (Skafte, 1997). Dr. Skafte proposes "that 'the shadow' may appear in unexpected places when the oracle is sought." Personality traits and genetic idiosyncracies are omnipresent. As is the dark side of our psyche (the shadow). Relying too much on oracular guidance can lead to a road that isn't conducive to spiritual needs. Something as unlikely as a bird flying into a neighborhood tavern, could set into motion a possible solution for a problem. Taking the bird's flight as an oracular sign post, one could meet an old drinking buddy he or she had not seen in a long time. Thinking the "oracle" has again provided guidance, a dependence on alcohol could follow a drinking spree in the bar.

As opposed to the personal unconscious, or analogous to society's ills influencing our behavior - namely addictive behavior, Jung's (1963) definition of the collective unconscious is suggestive:

> Although we human beings have our own personal life, we are yet in large measure the representatives, the victims and promoters of a collective spirit whose years are counted in centuries. We can well think all our lives long that we are following our own noses, and may never discover that we are, for the most part, supernumeraris on the stage of the world theater. There are factors which, although we do not know them, nevertheless influence our lives, the more so if they are unconscious.

With Jung's collective unconscious a likely contributor to addictive behavior, Ewen's (1989) description of Freud's reality and pleasure principles are also contributive.

> If Freud's reality principle, which delays the discharge of psychic tension until a suitable object has been found, doesn't operate, the Pleasure Principle (to achieve pleasure and avoid

unpleasure) does, because indulging in addictive behaviors produces pleasure. These principles can work with the Shadow - two separate areas of the psyche operating simultaneously. (p. 29).

The Shadow is the primitive and unwelcome side of personality that derives from our animal forbears. Unconsciously we project the Shadow onto other people. Here's an example by Johnson (1991):

> A young Japanese girl in a small village became pregnant. The villagers pressed her to name the father. After many angry words, she finally confessed. "It's the priest," she said. The villagers confronted the priest. "Ah so," was all he said. For months the people were down on the priest. Then a young man who had been away returned and asked to marry the girl. He was the father of the child. The girl accused the priest to protect him. The villagers then apologized to the priest. "Ah so," he said.

The girl projected her shadow onto the priest and the villagers. The wise priest kept silent and the problem worked out well for everyone concerned. This example demonstrates the Shadow in an environmental setting. Johnson also demonstrates this on a personal level using Marie Antoinette:

> The bored queen decided she wanted to touch something of the earth and ordered milk cows so she could become a milkmaid. After the cows' arrival she found this distasteful and changed her mind. The Queen's original impulse was correct: she needed something to balance the formality of her court. If she had continued as a milkmaid, the history of France might have been different. Instead she was beheaded.

Marie tried to balance her highly refined life with a peasant task, but she didn't see it through. If the shadow operates in the form of the addictive cycle for years of one's life, then stops through the recovery process, the constructive lifestyle afterwards can be a very rewarding experience for the individual and the village. Society and the addict benefit from the shadow.

Whether it is the more widely accepted causes discussed in part I or the causes gleaned from depth psychology, or a combination of each, there are considerably more dynamics involved; therefore, depth psychological perspectives should be investigated more vigorously. A spiritual awakening, which depth psychology can provide, can lead to wiser choices and a chance to become a more individuated human being.

Chapter Nine References

Alcoholics Anonymous World Services, Inc. 1991. *Alcoholics anonymous*. New York City: Alcoholics Anonymous World Services, Inc. p 544.

Alcoholics Anonymous World Services, Inc. 1984. *Pass it on: The story of Bill Wilson and how the A.A. message reached the world*. New York, NY: Alcoholics Anonymous World Services, Inc. p 383.

Bernards, Neal. (Ed.). 1988. *The mass media: Opposing viewpoints*. St. Paul, Minnesota: Greenhaven Press, Inc. p 210.

Bratter, Thomas E. & Forrest, Gary G. 1985. *Alcoholism and substance abuse: Strategies for   Clinical intervention*. New York: The Free Press. pp 14, 15, 77.

Cohen, Sidney M.D. *The chemical brain: The neurochemistry of addictive disorders*. Irvin, California: CareInstitute. p 57.

Ewen, Robert B. 1988. *An introduction to theories of personality*. Hillsdale, New Jersey: Lawrence Erlbaum Associates, Publishers. p 29.

Johnson, Robert A. 1991. *Owning your own shadow: Understnding the dark side of the psyche*. San Francisco: Harper. pp 38, 54.

Kinney, Jean M.S.W. & Leaton, Gwen. 1995. *Loosening the grip: A handbook of alcohol information*. St. Louis: Mosby. p 6, 80.

Nakken, Craig. 1988. *The addictive personality: Understanding compulsion in our lives*. San Francisco: Harper & Row. p 74.

Skafte, Dianne Ph.D. *Listening to the oracle: The ancient art of finding guidance in the signs and symbols all around us*. San Francisco: HarperCollins Publishers Inc. pp 3, 136

Woodman, Marion. 1982. *Addiction to perfection*. Toronto, Canada: Inner City Books. pp 9, 10, 52.

CHAPTER TEN

Transpersonal Psychology and the 12 Steps

In the course of a week approximately 15 million Americans will attend some kind of self-help group. Why is this happening? Because people have discovered that talking and listening to their fellow addicts has a soothing effect on the psyche, sometimes more so than doing the same thing in the presence of a therapist. "Support groups - a rather highfalutin name for what's usually nothing more than loosely structured gab sessions - salve psychological wounds, sometimes help destroy addictions and even extend the lives of people suffering from cancer and other physical afflictions" (Newsweek, Feb, 90).

In 1935 Bob Smith and Bill Wilson started Alcoholics Anonymous because one alcoholic talking to another had a therapeutic effect. If the meeting between those two alcoholics had not taken place there's no telling what kind of self-help alternative would be available today. In Transpersonal Psychology's stages of comprehension, we have the reactive stage, the physical stage, and the mental stage - the reactive stage would be the one that all people would be in if they weren't seeking help for their respective compulsions; therefore, consider how this world might be if all these people were placing the blame outwards for everything that happens to them, coping on just survival skills, continually talking about *me*, thinking of themselves as nothing, being controlled by the outside environment, and the countless other things that would be restricting their recovery. How many of those people would ever become individuated, or reach the mental stage of comprehension?

Having attended thousands of 12-step meetings, I do support 12-step programs, or any self-help group for that matter. However, while keeping in mind the multitudinous amount self-help groups and 12-step programs, my focus will be on Alcoholics and Narcotics Anonymous since they were the first. People helping people without professional intervention have proven, regardless of skepticism (including my own), that the professional community has indeed been awarded with help, because they couldn't handle it all by themselves - this is an indisputable fact. The title of James Hillman and Michael Ventura's (1992) dialogue, *We've Had a Hundred Years of Psychotherapy and the World's Getting Worse*, is a point worth considering.

I believe the concepts of intrinsic and extrinsic motivation apply here.

> INTRINSIC MOTIVATION occurs when there is no obvious external reward or ulterior motive behind your actions. (An ulterior motive is one which is over and above the apparent motive...for example an under the table payment for a charitable act.) The activity which is INTRINSICALLY motivated is mainly an end in itself. An action that is ALTRUISTIC is one which shows an unselfish concern for others, obviously with no material or monetary reward. Motivation is inner directed. EXTRINSIC MOTIVATION stems from obvious external factors such as pay, grades in school, rewards, obligations, or approval. Most 'work' is EXTRINSICALLY rewarded. However, it was found that large rewards for tasks done, often caused the person to lose interest in the task, according to research. When youngsters for example, were given large rewards for playing with marker pens, they soon lost interest in playing with them, compared to others who were not! Similar research proved out with college students. (Making Life Meaningful, p. 5).

We see people coming into 12-step programs who are obviously extrinsically motivated to be there. The court system has sent them, they're trying to salvage a marriage or a relationship, the doctor tells them *do or die*, and the list goes on. For the most part, these extrinsically motivated people will probably not recover. The people who are intrinsically motivated usually recover, because the desire to recover comes from within; they're sick and tired of being sick and tired. Myself included: I didn't want to spend any more time in institutions, I didn't want to suffer from any more hangovers, I didn't want to associate with people I couldn't trust, nor did I want to be continually chasing the bag; therefore, I found the only viable alternative - recovery. During my addiction, I found things outside of myself to be at fault - never within me.

For example, I was a bartender in a local biker bar where a lot of drug trafficking took place. On my night off I was there partying, dancing, etc. Two men came in that I had gotten to know over the previous couple of weeks or so, who established themselves as regular customers - we were on first name basis, and they asked if I could get them some drugs. I said no, that I didn't know where there was any. A couple hours later they asked again, and again I couldn't help them. About an hour before closing time they ask again, and this time I was able to get them some. I didn't even have to leave the bar. These two men were undercover agents. They didn't bust me on the spot because they didn't want to blow their cover, but when I came into the bar the next day for a drink, there they were, flashing their badges and asking me if I remembered them. The point I'm making here is my attitude. I felt that I was entrapped; in fact, I fought the case and lost with that as my defense. "It wasn't my fault, they tricked and badgered me into it!" Furthermore, since I wasn't actually selling drugs for profit, why should I be convicted for sales? I thought the judicial system really screwed me. It didn't occur to me that if I had not sold drugs to undercover cops, I wouldn't have gone to prison for selling drugs.

It now seems so obvious. A clear case of the Pythias Circle.

> In the PHYSICAL STAGE" (in transpersonal psychology) we mainly are operating under the rules of Classic or Operant Conditioning. We have a vague understanding of the Self, but it is not at all clear. If I am a victim, can do nothing, and I am always frustrated in what I do, why would I think I am a person who can do something? I don't. If I attempt to bring about change and change does not happen and this frustration is caused by person, place or thing OUTSIDE OF MY CONTROL, why would I feel anything but limited? I don't. The reason for this, is that my conditioning, which creates habit patterns that repeat "...with monotonous regularity" has no way of changing. The only way to get out of the trap is the motivation to move into the Mental Stage (Making Sense of Learning and Information Processing, p. 1).

I remember clearly at what point my recovery started, and I subsequently moved into the mental stage of development. After viewing a series of motivational tapes when I was in prison (Breaking Barriers), I began to understand how I was actually responsible for being in prison. I began to understand that literally everything I did, I did voluntarily, and that I had to be accountable for all of my actions. I had to monitor and discipline my thoughts, because I learned that "what we think, we are"; therefore, I didn't think about the bar where I used to work, I didn't think about the people I drank and used drugs with, I didn't think about drugs and alcohol in and of themselves, and when I did unconsciously start thinking about those things, I would rid myself of them and start thinking of places and people that I did want to be around when I was released.

> In the MENTAL STAGE all this can begin to change. When I am REFLECTIVE of my own Behavior, I can SELF-REFLECT as to what is going on. Only when I "Look Inward" and examine my own processes of thinking, believing or behaving, is there any possibility for me to DO ANYTHING ABOUT what I am thinking, believing, or my behavior? This is why we call it "THE BIRTH OF THE PERSON." Previous to this ability to Self-Reflect, we are constantly pointing our fingers at the outside as being the CAUSE or BLAME for all our problems or our difficulties or frustrations. If this is what I do, then by what logic or reasoning do I figure I HAVE ANYTHING WHATEVER TO DO WITH THE SITUATION? If I blame or say something OUTSIDE of myself is the cause or blame, then I have NOTHING TO DO with the outcome, change, difference, one way or another. When I Self-Reflect, USING MY INTELLECTUAL, LEFT BRAIN, MENTAL POWERS OF REASONING then and then alone is there a way out of the trap (Making Sense of Learning and Information Processing, P. 1).

"Fran Dory, previous executive director of the California Self-Help Center, recalls that when she was organizing groups in New York, a bunch of senior citizens trudged through a swirling blizzard and then, when an elevator failed to function, climbed 14 flights of stairs rather than miss their weekly meeting" (Newsweek, p. 54). There's nothing irrational about this kind of devotion. I know, because when I got out of prison I made three meetings a day. Two months later when I entered the local community college, I still made two meetings a day, and continued to do so for two years.

I believe it has to do with *how we see* the self-help phenomenon: Of primary importance in the study of any and all ideas is the role of the observer . . . you and I doing the study. Unless and until we have determined the means by which we comprehend reality, of whatever sort, there is a risk that we omit virtually the most important element of all, in any study of consciousness.

Here is an excellent definition of recovery by Gorski and Miller (1986):

> The recovery process is developmental. This means that recovery is a process of growth and development that progresses from basic to complex recovery tasks. This progression is from abstinence (learning how to stop using alcohol and/or drugs), to sobriety (learning how to cope with life without alcohol and/or drugs), to comfortable living (learning how to live comfortably while abstinent), to productive living (learning how to build a meaningful sober lifestyle) (p. 84).

To appropriately explain the self-help process, I'll start with the twelve steps of recovery: The explanation after each step is similar, but not verbatim, to what was covered about the steps in a previous paper, so by skipping this part, nothing will be lost toward understanding the premise of the paper.

Step One - we admitted we were powerless over our addiction – that our lives had become unmanageable.

The recovery process cannot start until we admit we have a problem and that our lives have indeed become unmanageable. Alcoholism and drug addiction, to many, is a problem that tells us we don't have a problem. One of the outstanding symptoms is "denial," so as long as we deny that we have a problem the recovery process is deadlocked. Who cares to admit complete defeat? Practically no one, of course. Every natural instinct cries out against the idea of being powerless. This is an awful thing to have to admit to; therefore, our admission of personal powerlessness finally turns out to be a firm bedrock upon which we can lead happy and purposeful lives.

Step Two - came to believe that a power greater than ourselves could restore us to sanity.

Some of us don't believe in God, others can't, and still others who do believe that God exists have no faith whatever that He will perform this miracle. A perfect example is me. I considered myself an atheist, then my sponsor asked me if I believed there was some kind of force in the universe other than ourselves. I could accept that there was. I had no idea what it was, and still don't, but I then started to open my mind to different theories; thus, it was possible for me to accept help in restoring my sanity from something outside of myself. Some people make the 12-step group their higher power, and others may have to use a light bulb or a tree. The point is, that most people have to recover with something other than self will; however, there are those who recover through spontaneous remission - basically, self will.

Step Three - made a decision to turn our will and our lives over to the care of God as we understood Him.

This step is one of willingness. Like all the remaining steps, this one calls for action, for it is only by action that we can cut away the self-will which has always blocked us from bringing a higher power into our lives. After accepting step three we can finally say: "God, (the universe, the allness, Allah, the tao, or whatever), "grant me the serenity to accept the things I cannot change, courage to change the things I can, and wisdom to know the difference" (Alcoholics Anonymous, p. 10).

Step Four - made a searching and fearless moral inventory of ourselves.

When a store clerk takes an inventory of merchandise, everything is added up, accounted for, and the damaged and/or expired goods are gotten rid of and the remaining goods are organized and stored. The same goes for a personal inventory. We need to find out who we are now that chemical substances are gone from our lives, so we add up the pluses and minuses. Coming to terms and acknowledging the things we've done in the past is no easy task; in fact, step four is one that requires continuous work, but we can continue with setting our mind at ease by accepting the good, as well as the bad, about ourselves. We also need to find exactly how, when, and where our natural desires have warped us. We need to look squarely at the unhappiness this has caused others and ourselves. By discovering what our emotional deformities are, we can move toward their correction. Without a searching and fearless moral inventory, most of us have found that the faith which really works in daily living is still out of reach. You see, 12-step programs aren't just a road to abstinence; it's more of a guide to happy and productive living. Therefore, thoroughness ought to be the key when taking inventory. It is wise to write out questions and answers. It will be an aid to clear thinking and honest appraisals. It will be the first tangible evidence of our complete willingness to move forward.

Step Five - admitted to God, to ourselves, and to another human being the exact nature of our wrongs.

The fourth and fifth steps are the biggies because in the fourth we had to list everything, but in the fifth we have to share it with another human being, whether it is our sponsor, clergyman, or just a friend. I heard a person at a meeting share once that he knew of a person that went to skid row with a bottle of wine and gave it to one of the wino's, then sat with him and poured his guts out. After he was finished, he thanked the wino for listening and left. Twelve-step programs teach us that we can't live alone with our problems, secrets, and the character defects which cause or aggravate them. This feeling of being at one with the universe, this emerging from isolation through the open and honest sharing of our burdens of guilt, brings us to a place where we may prepare ourselves for the following steps and a full and meaningful clean and sober life.

Step Six - were entirely ready to have God remove all these defects of character.

It has been said that this is the step that separates the men from the boys. Any person capable of enough willingness and honesty to try repeatedly step six on all his faults - without any reservations whatever - has indeed come a long way spiritually.

> Sure, I was beaten, absolutely licked. My own willpower just wouldn't work on alcohol. Change of scene, the best efforts of family, friends, doctors, and clergymen got no place with my

alcoholism. I simply couldn't stop drinking, and no human being could seem to do the job for me. But when I became willing to clean house and then asked a Higher Power, God as I understood Him, to give me release, my obsession to drink vanished. It was lifted right out of me (Twelve Steps and Twelve Traditions, p. 63).

The moment we say, "no, never!" our minds close against a higher power. Delay is dangerous, and rebellion may be fatal, so this is the point at which we abandon limited objectives, and allow our higher power (whatever that may be) to help.

Step Seven - humbly asked Him to remove our shortcomings.

This step specifically concerns itself with humility, for without it we can't remain abstinent. The seventh step is where we make the change in our attitude which permits us, with humility as our guide, to move out from ourselves toward others and the oneness of the universe. It is really saying to us that we now ought to be willing to try humility in seeking the removal of our other shortcomings just as we did in step two. If that degree of humility could enable us to find the universal spirit by which such a deadly obsession could be banished, then there must be hope of the same result respecting any other problem we could possibly have.

Step Eight - made a list of all persons we had harmed, and became willing to make amends to them all.

In order to live a happy life, clean and sober, we need to clear our conscience. We look backward and try to discover where we've been at fault, then make a vigorous attempt to repair the damage we've done. This isn't easy. It is a task which we may perform with increasing skill, but never really finish; in fact, it is suggested that we work these steps for the rest of our lives. When I committed myself to a clean and sober life and started attending 12-step meetings, the process began.

Step Nine - Made direct amends to such people wherever possible, except when to do so would injure them or others.

Making amends is not saying "I'm sorry" or apologizing. It's much more than that. If I were to approach someone I had done wrong to in the past, and asked him or her if there was anything I could do to right that wrong, and that person suddenly went off on me, told me where to stick my amends, etc., then I would leave and mark another amends off my list, because it isn't my job to see to it that my amends are accepted. I fulfilled my personal obligation to make an amends, and what that person does with it is their business. Above all, we should try to be absolutely sure that we are not procrastinating because of fear. For the readiness to take the full consequences of our past acts, and to take responsibility for the well-being of others at the same time, is what step nine is about.

Step Ten - continued to take personal inventory and when we were wrong promptly admitted it.

Taking inventories is a continual process - a life-long one, in fact. It's a good thing, too, because it really helps to figure things out when one writes it down and analyzes it. To just think about it usually isn't enough. We *constructively criticized* someone who needed it, when our real motive was to win a useless argument. We sometimes hurt those we love because they need to be *taught a lesson*, when we really want to punish them. Learning daily to spot, admit, and correct these flaws is the essence of character-building and good living.

Step Eleven - sought through prayer and meditation to improve our conscious contact with God as we understood him, praying only for knowledge of His will for us and the power to carry that out.

Personally, I don't recognize the word "God." I don't pray either; however, I believe I have a conscious contact with some unidentifiable something, which could be interpreted as "God" as I understand him. What this step is saying, is *Thy will, not mine, be done*. It is also suggesting prayer and meditation for those who are open to those mediums.

Step Twelve - having had a spiritual awakening as the result of these steps, we tried to carry this message to addicts and/or alcoholics, and to practice these principles in all our affairs.

There is a saying around 12-step programs: "We can't keep it unless we give it away." Here we experience the kind of giving that ask no rewards. When a practicing addict or alcoholic is down and out, drunk, hungry, broke, and destitute, and he reaches his or her hand out for help, it's our duty to help them; not enable, but help. We'll talk with them - not give them money, offer them food if they're hungry, offer them our experience, strength, and hope, and try to help them to recover. This is called twelve-step work, and as recovering addicts and alcoholics, we're obligated to do this any time we are called on to do so, whether it is in the middle of the night or the middle of the day - within reason of course. There are probably as many definitions of spiritual awakenings as there are people who have them, so there's really no specific way to define it except that one has now become able to do, feel, and believe that which he could not do before on his resources alone.

According to Gestalt theory, "learning is a cognitive phenomenon. In the learning process, there is a perceptual reorganization of the field. After learning has occurred, one sees the situation in a new light" (Theories and Systems of Psychology, p. 246). Obviously, the 12-step experience has been a learning process for me. It's also obvious that other types of self-help groups are a learning experience for many people. I think it's a good thing that so many people are finally able to get out of the physical stage of development and enter into the mental stage with the help of the self-help movement. However, since writing this paper, many of my opinions have changed, which is reflected in my book, *Scumbag Sewer Rats: An Archetypal Understanding of Criminalized Drug Addicts*, and in other papers in this book

111

Chapter Ten References

Gorski, Terence T. and Miller, Merlene. (1986). *Staying sober*. Independence, MO: Herald House/Independent Press.

Hillman, James and Ventura, Michael. (1993). *We've had a hundred years of psycotherapy and the world's getting worse*. San Francisco, Harper.

Lundin, Robert W. (1991). *Theories and systems of psychology*. Lexington, Mass: D.C. Heath.

Nitti, Louis. Transpersonal psychology. (Unpublished paper).

Nitti, Louis. Making sense of learning and information processing. (Unpublished paper).

Nitti, Louis. Making life meaningful.(Unpublished paper).

Wilson, Bill and Smith, Bob. (1976). *Alcoholics anonymous*. New York City: A.A. World Services.

Wilson, Bill and Smith, Bob. (1991). *Twelve steps and twelve traditions*. New York City: A.A. World Services.

CHAPTER ELEVEN

Critical Thinking

Critical thinking (sometimes referred to as directed thinking) is purposeful, reasoned and goal directed - it is thought and knowledge and the relationship between them. To break it down more, the critical component is the evaluation that is most often agreed upon, and thinking is obtaining the desired outcome. An ability to plan, have flexibility, be persistent, and have the willingness to self-correct are the characteristics of critical thinking essential for the recovering addict.

Thinking critically cannot be spontaneous; we don't get up in the morning and critically think our way through brushing our teeth, because we do that by second nature or habit. Recovering addicts (which include alcoholics) bring many of his or her old behaviors into recovery with them, and spontaneity in the form of hasty decisions is commonplace.

Memory
For recovering addicts, I think the best definition for memory is the recall of the past which involves learning; however, Random House Webster's dictionary defines it as: "The faculty or process of retaining or recalling past experiences" (p. 449). Including the word 'learning' in the first definition makes it apropos.

There are many mnemonic devices to aid memory. Acrostics are sentences created by words that begin with the first letters of a series of words. For example, "every good boy does fine," is the music student's acrostic for recalling the notes associated with the lines of a treble clef staff - EGBDF. Another one - one that normies (people whose never experienced addiction) might use when balking about drug addicts moving into their neighborhood, is NIMBY (not in my back yard). Rhymes and songs like the McDonald's song, "nobody can do it like

113

McDonald's can." Or how about, twiddly dee, twiddly dum, gimmy your dope or I'll get my gun. Just kidding. The loci system is a good one, which uses visual associations with locations that you already know. The peg system is another. It employs key words represented by numbers; for example, one is a bun, two is a shoe, three is a tree. The phonetic system is similar to the peg system, but instead of words representing numbers, sounds represent numbers. If recovering addicts would employ some of these methods instead of blowing them off after reading about them like most of them would do while in the throes of addiction, they'd stand a good chance of improving their memory. However, learning and implementing strategies for seemingly unimportant efforts is difficult for practicing addicts to do.

What we usually refer to as forgetting, is either the inability to recall stored information or the failure to store information in the first place. Recovering addicts, especially practicing addicts have what is often referred to as selective memory syndrome - that is, the failure to store information in the first place. The addict's attitude is - if the information isn't of any immediate use, then why make the effort to remember it?

Lucas (1990) explains a memory technique that he invented when he was a kid. He said that;

> ..when he went places with his parents in the car, one of the ways he would spend time burning up excess energy was to look at signs along the highway; for example, he saw an oil company sign that read SHELL, then he wondered to himself what that word would look like in alphabetical order, and he came up with EHLLS (p xi).

Psychologist Gordon Allport showed subjects a picture of a white man with a knife holding up a black man with a suit. This picture was presented in a flash to test the accuracy of their eyewitness testimony in a situation in which racial prejudice might influence their perception. How our memory can be influenced by biases, prejudices, and stereotypes should lead us to question ourselves periodically. The same scenario, of course, could be substituted with a man in a suit holding up a younger man with facial hair, a bald head, and tattoos.

Reasoning
Revlin and Mayer (1978) make a strong point:

> As people, we don't use the same psychological processes in finding conclusions required by the laws of formal logic or reasoning. Biases, prejudices and our emotions are some reasons why we're unable to do this. The notion of an irrational reasoner has been given reviewed interest as a result of the acceptance of categorical syllogisms into the social psychological literature as a diagnostic metric for assessing attitudes and beliefs. It is a frequent conclusion of such research with categorical syllogisms that the untrained reasoners are not strictly logical in their inferences and that they based their decisions primarily on personal knowledge and biases (p. 52).

Addicts can usually identify other addicts, and not only from the stereotypical observances such as shaved heads, tattoos, long hair, and/or their attire. Most addicts have a look that's in their facial expression, their walk - the way they carry themselves in general. All the other stereotypical nuances may not be there, but an addict can often recognize a fellow addict without them. Drug addicts are tricksters and are very adept at manipulation and persuasion; therefore, most of them don't believe they can be bamboozled (ya can't con a con). They're wrong about that because they're basing their decisions primarily on personal knowledge and biases. They doubt that the man with the *normie* appearance is capable of hoodwinking them, and you'll rarely hear them admit it when it happens. Let's have a look at some different types of reasoning given to us by Halpern (1989):

1. Inductive reasoning - If I have a situation where a statement has two premises, and the premises are logical, then I can find a valid conclusion through inductive reasoning (p. 126).

If every person you have ever seen has a drug habit, you would use this evidence to support the conclusion that everyone in the world has a drug habit. Obviously you can't be absolutely sure of this fact. It's always possible that someone you've never met does not have a drug habit. If you met just one person without a drug habit, then your conclusion must be wrong. So it is, with inductive reasoning, you can never prove that your conclusion is correct, but you can disprove it.

2. Deductive reasoning - With this type of reasoning, you would begin with statements known or believed to be true (p. 128).

A simple example would be the statement, "all drug addicts use drugs," then you could conclude that Billie Holiday, a woman you've never met, also uses drugs.

3. Syllogistic reasoning - In a nutshell, this is deciding whether a conclusion can properly be inferred from two or more statements. One type of syllogistic reasoning is categorical reasoning, which involves terms that tell us how many, like 'some,' 'none,' and 'all' (p. 128).

4. Probabilistic reasoning - is using information that we have to decide that a conclusion is likely true or likely not true. In everyday contexts, much of our reasoning is probabilistic. Likely the most intriguing is the circle diagrams and the five rules of categorical reasoning (p. 131). A more comprehensive discussion and examples of syllogistic and categorical reasoning are beyond the scope of this paper.

According to Halpern, "much of our thinking is like the scientific method of hypothesis testing. A hypothesis is a set of beliefs about the nature of the world; it is usually a belief about a relationship between two or more variables" (p. 223). There are several methods of testing hypotheses: inductive and deductive methods through operational definitions, independent and dependent variables, measurement sensitivity, populations and samples, and variability; furthermore, there are several ways to determine cause: isolation and control of variables, prospective and retrospective research, correlation and cause (which people frequently get confused), illusory correlation, validity, and reliability. I've learned to be aware of self-fulfilling prophecies in life as well as in learning to think critically. I am also quite convinced of the effectiveness of double-blind studies. In my previous life when I wrote and called in my own medical prescriptions, I became familiar with double-blind studies while researching pharmaceutical drugs for my personal use. Through a double-blind study I found that propoxyphene (Darvon) is less effective for pain than plain Aspirin. Perhaps because of this information, Darvon has been taken off the market.

Decision Making

Decision-making can be stressful, and it isn't limited to the uneducated: Whenever there is a simple error that most lay people fall for, there is always a slightly more sophisticated version of the same problem that experts fall for. I didn't write scrips only for mind-altering substances. I utilized my scam to provide prescription medication for me and my family. Obviously, a physician's expertise through experience would enable him to select more appropriate drugs than I did, even though I had a working knowledge of the Physician's Desk Reference.

Halpern remarks that "the availability heuristic is a rule of thumb we use to solve problems" (p.314). For example, when I read the question about whether there were more deaths due to homicide or due to diabetes-related diseases, and then read the answer (diabetes) and the reason why (the media), something clicked in my head. From now on, I thought, I'll probably be more aware of the effects of publicity. The media being in our face so much with all the murder and mayhem, homicide was naturally my choice. I was also fascinated that the availability of information in our memory will frequently determine the alternative selected in a decision-making process. In early recovery, if we have access, we need to go to meetings - a lot of them. When meeting time rolls around, sometimes we're faced with a decision - to go or not to go. Let's say the meeting I attended last night wasn't a very good one, but the availability of information in my memory concerns a money-making scheme. The alternative I select stands a good chance of being the one for money, even though I may not need money nearly as much as I do a meeting.

Many common myths inhibit recovering addicts from taking the essential steps for sound decision making; here are eight of them:

1. The future is a matter of chance or luck, so there's no use spending a lot of time and effort trying to make the best possible decision about something so trivial.

Isn't that something a practicing addict would think? Also, as I mentioned before, we bring a lot of our old thinking patterns into recovery with us, which is why there is such a high relapse rate.

2. Deadlines can't be changed.

3. Asking questions about an opportunity is asking for trouble.

This myth sounds rather ridiculous; however, especially in early recovery, our thinking is muddled and we're often overwhelmed.

4. Experts almost always agree. If you've asked one, you've asked them all.

Along with other defects of character, we often bring sloth into early recovery with us, so wouldn't it make sense to take the time and effort to do the research, rather than taking the word of one expert?

5. Consulting non-experts is pointless.

Whom are you going to trust - a drug and alcohol counselor who is a recovered addict, or a normie with a Ph.D. in clinical psychology? If you're an addict, all that education that the Ph.D. has is little comfort to the real world experience of the counselor.

6. If the members in your group of decision makers agree on the same choice without anyone dissenting, you can feel quite secure that it is a sound decision.

If it's a 12-step group, be aware that 12-step groups are not hot beds of mental health - they're recovering too. Sometimes we need to challenge the status quo. When I was teaching college courses, I encouraged my students to challenge the status quo–even challenge what I say (but don't get carried away), and challenge what's in text books. That is how innovation occurs. If we operate on nothing but present knowledge, then we stagnate, and nothing gets discovered.

7. If your opponents make unreasonable, exorbitant demands, there is no point in trying to negotiate.

8. Commitments are almost always irrevocable.

Don't make the mistake of misunderstanding this one. As long as we're not making a habit of breaking commitments, which most of us were when we were out there doing our thing, it's okay in recovery to break commitments if we give notice. It's not okay to leave people hanging.

All eight of these myths, as Revlin and Mayer (1980) point out, are difficult to discard because they are based on ideas that are sometimes valid (pp. 237, 239, 240, 241, 242, 243, 246, 248).

Problem Solving
A tendency in problem-solving, especially with addicts, is to pick the first solution that comes to mind and run with it. The disadvantage of this approach is that you may run off a cliff or into a worse problem than you started with. A better strategy in solving problems is to select the most attractive path from many ideas.

If I don't have a clue how to plan, then it wouldn't do me any good for someone to tell me to plan a solution. If I can't think of any solutions, then how am I going to generate and evaluate any? Halpern gives us strategies that can be used to help generate solutions. All of them won't work for everybody, but learning how to use different strategies can give us direction for problem solving. However, some of these strategies don't lend themselves as solutions for recovering addicts, but others are self-explanatory. I'll give some examples.

1. Means-Ends Analysis - When a goal is not immediately attainable, we often need to take detours to break the problem down into smaller problems, called subproblems, each with its own goal, called subgoals (p. 373).

Let's say that a concerned parent wants to help their son get out of the pits of addictive despair. This isn't an easy task, so the problem needs to be broken down into a smaller problem - say, learning about addiction. To solve this subproblem it will be necessary to set a goal - learn about dealing with addicts by going to Ala-non or Nar-anon, and work from there.

2. Working Backward - Whereas number one is a forward-looking strategy, sometimes it's better to plan your operations by working backward from the goal to your present or initial state (p. 375).

3. Simplification - A good way to approach problems is to strip away as much of the complexity as possible to reduce it to a simple form (p. 377).

When attending groups, say in a drug rehab, we're bombarded with solutions, techniques, and strategies to help keep us in recovery when we leave. We are told that we only need to change one thing - everything - but that's not going to happen overnight, so the best way to proceed is incrementally. Implement change slowly - one step at a time, and not allow ourselves to get overwhelmed.

4. Generalization and Specialization - When confronted with a problem, it is sometimes helpful to consider it as an example of a larger class of problems - generalization, or to consider it as a special case - specialization (p.380).

5. Random Search and Trial-and-Error - A truly random search would mean that there is no systematic order to which possible solutions can be explored. A trial and error search is best applied to well-defined problems with few possible solution paths (p. 381).

A random search for addicts usually means grasping for straws, which isn't an option that addicts should take. However, a trial and error process is within the grasp for addicts, and one that is self-explanatory.

6. Rules - Some kinds of problems, like series problems, depend on rules. Once the underlying principles are established, the problem is solved (381).

My example is very simple. If I am continually going to jail (a series of events) for violating the law, then I need to stop violating the law. Of course, if the problem is drug and/or alcohol oriented, then the problem is compounded, and a few other rules are in order.

7, Hints - Hints are additional information given after an individual has begun to work on a problem (p. 382).

8. Brainstorming - This one is fun - a method for group problem solving (p. 385).

9. Contradiction - This method works by showing that the goal could not possibly be obtained from the givens, since it is inconsistent with the givens (p. 386).

Whereas the description given above is vague, this simple example isn't. It's the problem of finding out if it is snowing. If you're indoors and a large overhanging roof prevents you from looking up, then look down to solve the problem.

10. Restate the Problem - This is a useful strategy for ill-defined problems. In well defined problems, the goal is usually explicitly stated in unambiguous terms that leave little room for restatement (p. 386).

Recovering addicts often ask: "How can I save money?" They shop in discount markets, cut coupons out of newspapers, cut back on gas, and spend their weekends at home rather than going out. Suppose you restate the problem so that it becomes: "How can I have more money?" Their solutions then change to things like, getting a higher paying job or moving to where rent is cheaper.

11. Analogies and Metaphors - Mythology and fairy tales have been assisting the human condition for hundreds of years (p. 387).

We can draw on alchemy for this one. The prima materia (primal material) in the alchemical vessel has to be destroyed (killed) before the transformation process can start taking place. Think of the old addicted self as the prima materia that has to be killed, and the new recovered self as the finished product. With me, I've used this one by referring to my years of active addiction as my first life, and the years of being clean and sober as my second life.

12. Consult an Expert (p. 389) - Self explanatory

Creative Thinking
The notion of unusual or unique, and the notion of good or useful, is what is involved in creativity. It always involves judgement, and people may not agree on which actions or outcomes deserve to be labeled creative.

Not all creative people are alike either, which makes defining creativity a challenge and assessing it a monumental undertaking. The traditional psychological definition of creativity includes two parts: originality and functionality. You can't be creative unless you come up with something that hasn't been done before. The idea has to work, or be adaptive or functional in some way; it has to meet some criteria of usefulness. There is a distinction to be made between creativity (lower case c) and Creativity (upper case C): creativity, which is often used as an indicator of mental health, includes every day problem-solving and the ability to adapt to change. Creativity, on the other hand, is far more rare. It occurs when a person solves a problem or creates an object that has a major impact on how other people think, feel, and live their lives. Mere creativity implies basic functionality. Creativity is something for which we give Pulitzer and Nobel Prizes.

For those interested, I improved this paper and imported it into my book, *Scumbag Sewer Rats: An Archetypal Understanding of Criminalized Drug Addicts*.

Chapter Eleven References

Braham, Carol C. (Ed). *Random house webster's dictionary*. (1998). New York, Ballantine Books.

Halpern, Diane F. (1989) *Thought and knowledge*. Hillsdale N.J.: Lawrence Erlbaum Ass.

Lahey, Benjamin B. (1989) *Psychology: An introduction*. Dubuque, Iowa: Wm C. Brown.

Lorayne, Harry and Lucas, Jerry. (1990) *The memory book*. New York: Ballantine Books.

Revlin, Russell and Mayer, Richard E. (1978) *Human reasoning*. Washington D.C.: V.H. Winston & Sons.

Wheeler, Daniel D. and Janis, Irving L. (1980) *A practical guide for making decisions*. New York, The Free Press.

CHAPTER TWELVE

Freud: Genius or Deviate

Was Sigmund Freud a twisted, deranged, sexual pervert with no evidence to support his theories? Or was he a competent physician, an effective psychiatrist, a brilliant theorist, and a creative professional exploring and developing new concepts? The answer to these questions is yes. He was, but he was also a neurotic drug addict and was probably psychologically disturbed sexually. Ferris (1997) explains Freud as having;

> ..a fluttering heart and burning pains in the chest, which made him into a hypochondriac; he was taking cocaine and smoking heavily; aged thirty-nine, he was convinced he would be dead at fifty-one, a date that had mysterious significance. He knew he was neurotic (p. 7).

Bych (1974) quotes Freud himself: "A few minutes after taking cocaine, one experiences a sudden exhilaration and a feeling of lightness" (p. 58), then he goes on to explain physiological symptoms in the palate. Here's Ferris again who writes that;

> ..long after Freud's death his daughter Anna, the guardian of his memory, was encouraging friends to keep quiet about the cocaine story. Ernest Jones wrote about Freud's habit but played down its extent. In a private letter of 1952 to James Strachey, Freud's translator, he said that 'the way Freud thrust the cocaine on everybody must have made him quite a menace ...he was only interested in the magical effects of the drug, of which he took too much himself' (p. 59).

I've established peremptorily that Freud was a neurotic cocaine user. Now check out what else Ferris has to say concerning Freud's sexuality: "a series of dreams, forty years after the events he hoped to recall, was devoted to her. Freud concluded that the servant had been 'my teacher in sexual matters', though he failed to explain what he meant" (p. 16). Ferris also quotes Freud concerning sexual perversion: "Unfortunately, my own father was one of these perverts and is responsible for the hysteria of my brother (all of whose symptoms are identifications) and those of several younger sisters (p. 135).

Bettelheim (1983) informs us that "for years Freud had lived in virtual seclusion, largely because of the development of a cancer of the mouth which caused him great pain" (introduction). The pain he was in required attention; consequently, he became addicted to morphine and cocaine. Pain and drugs can, and often do transform the mental and emotional balances of the mind.

Sigmund Freud was an Austrian physician who, among other things, developed psychoanalysis. He won recognition as a great psychological leader, and was the first to map the unconscious world of the human mind. Freud also listed three main forces in a human's life: the id, an instinctive force; the ego, an executive force that contacts the world of reality; and the super ego, the superior disciplinary force. He conceived the Oedipus complex, which is the unconscious sexual attachment a male child has to his mother. In females, it's the Electra complex, which entails penis envy. This is where so many people think Freud was crazier than most of his patients, because none of us like to think of ourselves, or our children, as having thoughts of incest. Psychologist Karen Horney, however, felt it was neither normal nor universal, and that when it does occur, it is a neurotic relationship fostered by provocative behavior on the part of the parent. Freud also emphasized, over-emphasized actually, the importance of sex overall in human behavior.

Holt states that;

> ..the idea has gone abroad that the term 'Freudian' is somehow synonymous with 'sexual,' and that to read Freud's own works would be fairly to immerse oneself in the licentious and the illicit. This belief, which makes the mention of Freud so alluring to some and so disconcerting to others, is as ill-founded as it is widespread (p. vi).

124

Sigmund Freud stirred the emotions of many people - past and present, but the fact remains that his contribution to the field of psychology is extensive, which should arouse anyone's imagination concerning where psychology would be today without his contribution. It is the opinion of many, even some of Freud's fellow psychologists, that some of his theories were warped and demented. Maybe they were, but it cannot be dismissed that he made a significant contribution to the field of psychology, and many of those very theories inspired the groundwork for reams of psychological material available to us today.

Having many other accomplishments to his credit, it's difficult to discount Freud's theories, even on sexuality: After the publication of *Studies in Hysteria* in 1885 in which Freud collaborated with a man named Breuer, he turned to the analysis of dreams, and in 1900 (1899 actually, but he wanted the copyright date to read 1900), he published Interpretation of Dreams. Except for his collaboration with Breuer, Freud, for more than a decade, stood completely isolated from the medical community, and when not completely ignored, his theories were the objects of ridicule. It was not until 1902 that several young doctors began to gather around him with the intention of learning and practicing psychoanalysis, and from this group grew the Viennese Psycho-Analytic Society. By 1908 Freud had colleagues throughout Europe, including Carl Jung, Alfred Adler, Ernest Jones, Brill, Ferenczi, Sadger, Stekel, and Wilhelm Reich, among others. In that same year the first International Congress of psycho-analysis was held at Salzburg. In the following year, at the invitation of Clark University, Freud visited the United States and gave five lectures on his discoveries, which were later published as the Origin and Development of Psycho-Analysis.

Here's a quote from one of Freud's lectures:

> One thing, at least, I may pre-suppose that you know - namely, that psychoanalysis is a method of medical treatment for those suffering from nervous disorders; and I can give you at once an illustration of the way in which psycho-analytic procedure differs from, and often reverses, what is customary in other branches of medicine. Usually, when we introduce a patient to a new form of treatment, we minimize its difficulties and give him

confident assurances of its success. This is, in my opinion, perfectly justifiable, for we thereby increase the probability of success. But when we undertake to treat a neurotic psychoanalytically, we proceed otherwise. We explain to him the difficulties of the method, its long duration, the trials and sacrifices which will be required of him; and, as to the result, we tell him that we can make no definite promises, that success depends upon his endeavors, upon his understanding, his adaptability and his perseverance. We have, of course, good reasons, into which you will perhaps gain some insight later on, for adopting this apparently perverse attitude (The Great Books of the Western World - Freud. p. 449).

With the establishment of the International Psycho-Analytic Association in 1910, Freud devoted his efforts with increasing success to the development of the psychoanalytic movement. Disagreement later led to a severance of relations between Freud and several of his closest associates, including Adler, Stekel, Rank, and Jung, but Freud was the acknowledged founder of psychoanalysis and the leader of the movement. So, as previously stated, some of Freud's colleagues felt he was off track with some of his theories.

Bettleheim (19183) asserts that;

The English translations of Freud's writings not only distort some of his central concepts, but actually make it impossible for the reader to recognize that Freud's ultimate concern was man's soul, the basic element of our common humanity. And it is shown that these translations, by masking much of the essential humanism of Freud's work, have led to a tragic misunderstanding and widespread misuse of Freud's work.

Freud was an asset to the field of psychology, but some of his theories were viewed, and still are, as less than reliable. Very possibly his physical affliction and pain and consequent drug addiction, not to mention his childhood issues with sexuality, contributed to some of his deviant theories. At any rate, everybody has the right to their own opinion, and mine is that psychology - for good or bad - wouldn't be what it is today without the contribution and works of Sigmund Freud.

Chapter Twelve References

Adler, Mortimer J. (1952). The great books of the western world - Freud. Chicago: William Benton.

Bettelheim, Bruno. (1983). *Freud and man's soul*. New York: Alfred A. Knopf.

Bych, Robert. (1974). *Cocaine papers*: Sigmund Freud. New York: New American Library.

Ferris, Paul. (1997). *Dr. Freud: A life*. Washington, D.C.: Counterpoint.

Holt, Edwin B. (1915). *The Freudian wish and it's place in ethics*. New York: Henry Holt.

CHAPTER THIRTEEN

Psychological Theories

Sigmund Freud

When I think of Freud in relation to addictive behavior, the id, ego, and superego come to mind. The id is hedonistic - sleazy, fun-loving and pleasure seeking. The id says, "John, use that money to buy bag of dope and then share it with *her*. You'll surely get laid for your generosity." The superego is the id's opposite - the holier-than-thou doppelganger with impeccable moral and ethical standards. The superego counters the id by saying, "John, you must not betray your inner goodness. That dope is evil, and using her in that way is immoral. The ego (our conscious self) is the mediator. The ego might say, "I believe I'll compromise. I get the bag of dope and forget her. That leaves more dope for me anyway." I like Freud's analogy; in fact, many other theorists do too, they just clothe it in different terminology.

Concerning sexuality, Freud felt we are driven by the pleasure principle. He put much emphasis on this. In some ways I agree with him, but not to the extreme he does. After all, continuing the species is innate; therefore, sexuality is innate. Freud takes some of his theories out to left field. For example, Ferris (1997) tells us that "in 1897 he had confided his view to Fliess that all addictions, to alcohol, morphine, tobacco, or anything else, were only substitutes for the 'primary addiction', masturbation" (p. 342.). That's a strange thing for a man to say who was addicted to morphine and cocaine.

Freudian theory says we have defense mechanisms used by the ego to ward off threats from the id and the superego, or the external world, and therefore reduces the corresponding anxiety. I concur, for during my addiction I used a few defense mechanisms myself.

Freud (1961) regards religion as extremely harmful to the individual and to society. He said that since people are indoctrinated with religion during childhood, before they are able to apply reason to the whole issue, they become dependent on its narcotizing effects. Freud also said that a believer is bound to the teachings of religion by certain ties of affection (p. 59).

Overall I agree that Freud was a pathological mess; however, his contributions of the unconscious, dream interpretation, psychoanalysis, defense mechanisms, only to mention a few, are indispensable to the evolution of psychology. The fact that he was a major influence undeniable.

Carl Jung

As a protégé of Freud, some of Jung's theories were considered outlandish: the occult, ESP, alchemy, and the myth of flying saucers; therefore, in ways, his theories were even more controversial than Freud's, and easy to dismiss as absurd and unscientific. Personally, I think it's the other way around, but that's because I am a Jungian psychologist. I've had a lot of course work espousing Jungian theories, but I wasn't exposed enough to the occult to make an objective opinion. I wouldn't categorize flying saucers as myth, like many people do; the way I see it, it's absurd to think that human beings are the most, or the only, intelligent life form in the universe capable of space travel.

As with all the theorists discussed forthwith, the scope of this work cannot touch on everything that they're credited with, especially Freud and Jung. The collected works of Jung consist of 22 volumes, and that's not all of it.

Jung's theory of the archetypes (the collective unconscious) is where I focused my doctoral research. My dissertation is entitled *Scumbag sewer rats: Criminalized male drug addicts and the trickster archetype.* In that work I also expound on the archetype of the *puer aeternus* (Latin for eternal boy). To read my work on the archetypes personified in drug addicts, read my book *Scumbag Sewer Rats: An Archetypal Understanding of Criminalized Drug Addicts.*

When considering the breadth of his writing, I was and still am struck by the practical wisdom of the following words by Jung (1953):

Anyone who wants to know the human psyche will learn next to nothing from experimental psychology. He would be better advised to put away his scholar's gown, bid farewell to his study, and wander with human heart through the world. There, in the horrors of prisons, lunatic asylums and hospitals, in drab suburban pubs, in brothels and gambling-hells [sic], in the salons of the elegant, the Stock Exchanges, Socialist meetings, churches, revivalist gatherings and ecstatic sects, through love and hate, through the experience of passion in every form in his own body, he would reap richer stores of knowledge than text-books a foot thick could give him (Jung, 1953, p. 244 [CW 7, para. 409]).

Without going into detail, since I've discussed it in an earlier paper in this volume, Jung was instrumental is the development of Alcoholics Anonymous, mainly his contribution of spiritual experience which is one of the cornerstones of AA and other 12-step programs today.

Alfred Adler
Another protégé of Freud, Adler preferred practical recommendations for dealing with one's problems, bringing up children, getting along with others, and upgrading the quality of life in general. He also argued that people have an innate potential for relating to others. This social interest involves more than membership in a particular group. It refers to a sense of kinship with humanity, and it enables our species to survive through cooperation.

I agree that if one fails to give a child sufficient care and attention, it creates the belief that the world is a cold and unfriendly place. And what better way to set the stage for a defense mechanism that can often endure for the rest of their lives? Among others, addiction often serves as a defense mechanism, shielding the pain and suffering of the insufficient care and attention during childhood.

A lifestyle can be revealed by a person's physical movements. Always leaning on something may reflect dependency and a need for protection. Slouching, trembling, remaining a distance from other people, avoiding eye contact, or sleeping in a fetal position may indicate cowardly tendencies. Body language is a language, a communication. We see this with addicts, in the way they carry themselves. Now anybody can spot the obvious ones whose heads are shaved, have facial hair, and are sporting tattoos and/or various body piercings. I'm talking about a subtle look that usually only other addicts can detect. And the same goes with jointsters (ex- cons) - they wear certain characteristics, and other jointsters can usually spot it regardless of how hard they try to conceal it.

Adler (1964) says that;

> Neurosis originates in the first few years of life, influenced by such factors as pampering. Pampered people are not in good repute. They never were. Parents are not fond of being accused of pampering. The spoiled person himself refuses to be regarded as such. Again and again a doubt occurs as to what we mean by pampering. But, as though by intuition, everyone feels it as a burden and an obstacle to proper development (p. 144).

I disagree - maybe some neuroses originate in the first few years of life, but many definitely develop later. For example, neuroses stemming from substance abuse, for the most part, come later in life.

Karen Horney

Horney, yet another protégé of Freud, says that neurotics sell their souls to the devil by abandoning their real desires and capacities in favor of the idealized image. Lending myself as an example that I'm sure all addicts can identify with to some degree, is the idealized image of being cool. Growing up, most boys of my generation, wanted to be a policeman, fireman, school teacher, whatever. However, at some point we were impressed by someone who was cool, and it was then that something happened that later turned into an addictive personality, often starting with the coolness associated with smoking cigarettes. Yes, I'm saying that for many, cigarettes are a gateway to chemical substances, sometimes sooner, but usually later in life.

Horney (1967) defines the neurotic need for love succinctly: "While it is important to the healthy person to be loved, honored, and esteemed by those whom he esteems or on whom he is dependent, the neurotic need for love is compulsive and indiscriminate" (p. 246.). In support of her contention, it's my contention that the prevention of a neurotic need for love is contingent on how much love was lavished on one during their childhood years.

Horney believed that patients may expect great gains from psychotherapy without having to work at their problems. I've found this to be true in the recovery process from addiction. Many addicts enter the recovery process to improve their neurotic behavior associated with their addiction, but so many of them want to do it without having to change.
While at the same time I feel that psychoanalysis is effective, I also concur with Horney when she encourages patients to engage in self-analysis. She warns that an overemphasis on childhood events may encourage patients to wallow in the memory of past hurts, thereby rationalizing their failure to work at the task of therapy. Also, patients actively defend their neurotic solutions - in my case addiction, and deny the existence of their inner conflicts, avoid the frightening prospect of change, and cling to the only apparently successful mode of adjustment that they have ever known. It was definitely easier for me to take a fix or get drunk than to deal with life in any other way, especially if it required a lot of time and effort.

Erich Fromm
Positive growth of a child is facilitated by parents who are warm, affectionate, and nonthreatening. But if the sense of self-reliance should be damaged by pathogenic parental behaviors, the child is likely to sacrifice its innate healthy potentials and seek to escape. I said the same thing in different words in response to Horney's neurotic need for love. Pathogenic parental behaviors include pessimism, joylessness, narcissism, rigidity, necrophilia, and physical abuse. And I'll add drug addiction to that list.

Fromm says that loving parents are the exception, rather than the rule. It is a nauseating and staggering statistic that 95% of the families in this country are dysfunctional in one way or another. Of course, how the word dysfunctional is defined can alter those statistics considerably.

The goal of a clinical psychologist is not to define and treat a set of symptoms, but to understand the neurotic character and the resulting difficulties in living. It's like going to 12-step meetings, we don't go there only to find out how not to drink or use drugs, which is what is commonly believed. I spent more than thirty years practicing my addiction; therefore, I found that to recover, I had to unlearn old coping strategies to learn how to live anew.

As Fromm (1976) points out,

> Our judgements are extremely biased because we live in a society that rests on private property, profit, and power as the pillars of its existence. To acquire, to own, and to make a profit are the sacred and unalienable rights of the individual in an industrial society. What the sources of property are does not matter; nor does possession impose any obligations on the property owners. The principle is: Where and how my property was acquired or what I do with it is nobody's business but my own; as long as I do not violate the law, my right is unrestricted and absolute (p. 69).

It's a shame, but this is the way most people in our society are. I'm glad that material possessions do not take top priority in my life. I'd rather *Be* than *Have*. With that said, it hard to discount how the *Have* can make life more comfortable.

Harry Stack Sullivan

'Malevolent transformation' is a distortion or warp in personality development, resulting in the irrational belief that other people are enemies and has no tenderness or love to give, caused by insufficient maternal tenderness and excessive parental hostility, irritability, and anxiety during the childhood stage. This is the same thing that Horney and Fromm said, but clothed in different words.

Lundin (1991) considers Sullivan's idea of the 'self-system' as;
> ..an organized perception of one's own self, including the desirable 'good-me' and undesirable 'bad-me.' Results from experiences with one's body and the reflected opinions of significant others, has the primary goal of reducing anxiety. The security operations of the self-system also create the impression that we differ more from others than is actually the case (a delusion of unique individuality), and may even result in a

grandiose self-personification somewhat like the Adlerian superiority complex (p. 337-338).

From my experience, I can say that grandiosity is typical of many addicts I have associated with, not to mention the many I was merely acquainted with. The irony of that observation is an oxymoron–a grandiose and egotistical self-image coupled with low self esteem.

Sullivan says that psychotherapy is primarily a form of education, rather than a medically oriented "cure." I also see it that way. It takes the "psychotherapist" off the pedestal.

Erik Erikson
Another protégé of Freud, Erikson was only a mediocre student, and he never earned a university degree of any kind, but his credibility is well established with one of the most widely accepted models of human development.

Although Erikson retains Freud's structural model, he also cautions against such concepts as id, ego, and superego. He stresses that these are designed to facilitate the discussion and understanding of personality, rather than establish entities located within the psyche.

Erikson remarks that the identity crisis proves to be so troublesome that neither a primarily positive or negative identity can be achieved, the individual may reject the demands of adulthood and extend the adolescent stage well past the appropriate age. This remark is clothing the problem of the *puer aeternus* with his own words.

"To Erikson, adolescence is not an affliction," says Roazen (1976), "but a normative crisis, i.e., a normal phase of increased conflict characterized by a seeming fluctuation in ego strength as well as by a high growth potential" (p. 90).

Erikson was one of the first analysts to treat children, devising valuable techniques of play therapy. He did stray a little from Freud when seeking to avoid some potential biases in Freudian therapy by using face-to-face interviews, rejecting transference neurosis, and avoiding a preoccupation with the patient's past.

The identity crisis, play therapy, his study of psychosocial influences on personality development, and his prize winning study of Gandhi are his biggest contributions.

Gordon W. Allport
Allport believed that most adult motives consist of cognitive processes that are relatively independent of biological drives; for example, Kamikaze pilots during World War II followed the manifestly unpleasurable course of sacrificing their lives for their country. Instances like this lead Allport to conclude that much of adult behavior can't be explained in terms of drive reduction.

Allport is the first theorist who devised a written questionnaire to measure such constructs as values. Values are important and make up quite a bit of who we are. Recovering addicts need to unlearn most of their old values and develop a whole new set of them, or recapture the ones that were hopefully instilled during their early development.

Allport describes the personality in terms of traits: friendliness, ambitiousness, cleanliness, enthusiasm, seclusiveness, punctuality, shyness, talkativeness, dominance, submissiveness, generosity, prejudice, and so forth. He estimates that there are some 4,000 to 5,000 traits and 18,000 trait names.

Allport (1954) justifies the normality of prejudgment (prejudice):

> Everywhere on earth we find a condition of separateness among groups. People mate with their own kind. They eat, play, reside in homogeneous clusters. They visit with their own kind, and prefer to worship together. Much of this automatic cohesion is due to nothing more than convenience. There is no need to turn to out- groups for companionship. With plenty of people at hand to choose from, why create for ourselves the trouble of adjusting to new languages, new foods, new cultures, or to people of a different educational level? It requires less effort to deal with people who have similar presuppositions (p. 17).

This may have been more widely accepted in 1954, and it's not nonexistent today, but with widespread issues concerning diversity and multi-cultural relations, Allport's stand on prejudgement today isn't as relevant.

The healthy individual usually confronts the various difficulties in life and is guided by motives that are conscious, flexible, and autonomous. But the neurotic or psychotic, whose predisposition for normal development has been blocked by pathogenic influences, escapes important problems through self-deceiving defense mechanisms and is dominated by motives that are unconscious, compulsive, and childish. As a result, the pathological individual is too self-centered and fearful to achieve the balanced give and take required for meaningful interpersonal relationships. Here's the *puer* again wrapped in Allport clothing. Or, I guess you could say, here's Allport's theory wrapped in *puer* clothing, for the *puer* universally escapes important problems through self-deceiving defense mechanisms, is dominated by motives that are unconscious, and is compulsive, childish, and self-centered.

Carl R. Rogers
A person will resort to various distortions and denials (as in addiction). But in the safety of the therapeutic situation, also in 12 step meetings, he or she is able to accept these anxiety- provoking aspects of experience, realize that it is the self-concept that must be changed, and reorganize it appropriately.

I acknowledge this in my book, *Scumbag Sewer Rats*. I state there that it is my contention that the general public, the mental health profession, the American judicial system, and criminalized drug addicts themselves are struck with a social paradigmatic attitude toward criminalized drug addicts that characterizes them as dirty, rotten, scumbag sewer rats.

Rogers' (1970) work on encounter groups, and the following quote is quite illustrative of what I've found true in 12 step meetings:

> Closely allied with the foregoing is the need for encounter groups to bridge the so-called generation gap. In groups where there has been a wide spread of age, it has not been found that these age differences are of any significance once the group process really begins to operate (p. 141).

What Ewen (1988) says concerning Rogers, is that;

> A constructive therapeutic relationship depends in part on the client perceiving the therapist as genuine, or in touch with his or her own inner experience and able to share it when appropriate. To withhold one's self as a person and to deal with the client as an object does not have a high probability of being helpful. It does not help to act calm and pleasant when actually I am angry and critical. It does not help to act as though I know the answers when I don't. It doesn't help to try to maintain any facade, to act in one way on the surface when I am experiencing something different underneath. Instead, I have found that the more that I can be genuine in the relationship, the more helpful it will be. This means that I need to be aware of my own feelings, in so far as possible, and willing to express them (p. 386).

Depth psychology leans heavily on mythological motifs. For example, if psychotherapists behave in too dignified a way in therapy, then how can they help the many clients who come to the therapist in the first place to discuss the undignified aspects of their lives. Only the undignified Hermes exemplified in the therapist can constellate a communication with the undignified side of life and can evaluate hermetically what has been reported as undignified. And so it is with addicts who are seeking recovery. Addicts will not cooperate with a therapist who doesn't have at least some kind of emotional tie with addiction. Preferably the therapist is a recovered addict.

Abraham H. Maslow
Maslow's self-actualization, according to Goble (1970),

> ..is prominent only in older people. The young are more concerned with issues like education, identity, love, and work, which Maslow regards as preparing to live. As self-actualized people are usually sixty years of age or more, most people do not belong in this category; they are not static, they have not arrived; they are moving toward maturity. The actualization process means the development or discovery of the true self and the development of existing or latent potential (pp. 24, 25).

Maslow, therefore, refers to the needs of self-actualizing individuals as metaneeds, among which are a love of beauty, truth, goodness, justice, and usefulness. Self-actualizing individuals have strong moral and ethical standards.

As a depth psychologist, I have internalized the same ideas, but clothed in the language of depth psychology. Self actualization translates into Individuation, the goal in Jungian psychoanalysis: Individuation is a process informed by the archetypal ideal of wholeness, which in turn depends on a vital relationship between ego and unconscious. The aim is not to overcome one's personal psychology or to become perfect. Thus individuation involves an increasing awareness of one's unique psychological reality, including personal strengths and limitations, and at the same time a deeper appreciation of humanity.

As discussed in an earlier paper, my alchemical approach to recovery results in the individuation of the recovery process–the Gold, or the philosopher's stone. Again another restatement in different terminology.

Rollo May

> Each of us has an inherent need to exist in the world into which we are born, and to achieve a conscious and unconscious sense of ourselves as an autonomous and distinct entity. The stronger this being-in-the-world or 'Dasein,' the healthier the personality. According to May our dynamic being-in-the-world comprises three interrelated modes: biological drives (Umwelt), relationship to others (Mitwelt), and the affirmation of one's self and values (Eigenwelt) (p. 128).

May accepts Freud's contention that paying for one's therapy helps to overcome difficulties. If a person doesn't benefit from therapy when he pays for it, he'll most likely benefit less if it's given to him without a monetary obligation. This contradicts the success of 12-step programs, for it is their credo that, "we can't keep it unless we give it away."

B. F. Skinner

Skinner (1974) explains that;

a newborn baby knows how to cry, suckle, and sneeze. We say that a child knows how to walk and how to ride a tricycle. The evidence is simply that the baby and child exhibit the behavior specified. Moving from verb to noun, we say that they possess knowledge, and the evidence is that they possess behavior. It is in this sense that we say that people thirst for, pursue, and acquire knowledge (p. 137).

This is a description of behaviorism broken down to its fundamental basics. Skinner 'is' behaviorism; however, he thought that different techniques should be used with those problems for which they are especially well suited, such as: desensitization for a fear of examinations, assertive training for a client inhibited with members of the opposite sex, or various procedures in combination. These variations of treatment are limited to behavior therapy.

Skinner attributes religious belief primarily to an accident of birth, namely the conditioning imposed by one's parents, or by the religious school to which they belong. Many religions try to control behavior by claiming some connection with supernatural forces, which presumably punish behaviors defined by the religion as immoral (as with the threat of Hell) and reward behaviors defined as moral (as with the promise of Heaven). When sinful behavior is in fact emitted, these religions offer powerful reinforcement in the form of absolution. Other religions do not appeal to the supernatural, and simply reinforce, with approval, those behaviors that they deem to be virtuous, like the *golden rule*. But whatever the form, religion is to Skinner, and Freud, and myself, for I agree completely, is merely another example of behavior control through conditioning.

John Dollard and Neal E. Miller
Cohen (1977) states that;

> The more we learn about the brain, the more we appreciate that it is one of the most wonderful miracles in the universe. To try to understand the brain is an infinitely challenging goal worthy of Man's highest humanistic and aesthetic aspirations. This quest does not need to be justified by any practical social consequences, although it certainly has them. None of the

people I know who are enamored with trying to understand the brain are concerned with what to do with their leisure time, or plagued with boredom, a sense of futility or the meaninglessness of their existence (p. 241).

I suppose this, among other things, is why I study psychology.

The researcher, in Dollard's (1937) opinion,

> ..cannot always be sure that the book he starts to write is the one that will be given him to finish. My original plan was to study the personality of Negroes in the South, to get a few life histories, and to learn something about the manner in which the Negro person grows up. It was far from my wish to make a study of a community, to consider the intricate problem of the cultural heritage of the Negro, or to deal with the emotional structure of a specific small town in the deep South. I was compelled, however, to study the community, for the individual life is rooted in it (p. 1).

I've included this because I identify with it so much. During the course of my writing, this phenomenon has repeatedly surfaced. In my doctoral studies I started writing about the *puer*, and ended up with a dissertation written primarily about the trickster, and then published a book focusing on both the *puer* and the trickster.

To some psychologists, Dollard and Miller's attempted rapprochement between behaviorism and psychoanalysis contains much interest and importance. Thus they have been praised for emphasizing and clarifying two particularly important variables, anxiety and conflict, and for their non-metaphysical definition of repression.

Albert Bandura

Bandura is highly critical of the extent to which television and other media portray violent behavior, since these are all too likely to serve as models (especially in the case of children). I couldn't agree more and there's no shortage of research substantiating his position. I'd bet my little finger that the reason so much violence rests on the money it generates, mainly at the box office. Thus, he urges such controls as a privately funded board that would try to sway public opinion against media violence, and in favor of programs that are nonviolent and informative, such as the well-known Sesame Street. I agree; in fact, more than children are being influenced by the violence portrayed on television and other media: Bandura brought children into a laboratory and had them observe an adult repeatedly hitting an inflated Bobo doll about three feet tall. Bandura wondered to what extent the children would copy the adult's behavior. The children did copy the adult's behavior extensively, and many of them, I'm certain, took that behavior into adulthood with them. So, it would be hard to deny that the influence of media, with all the drinking and drug use being presented, would increase the odds for widespread addiction.

James Hillman

Hillman is a psychologist and is considered to be one of the most original thinkers of the 20th century. He trained at the Jung Institute in Zurich under Jung, and subsequently developed the field of archetypal psychology. Hillman is a prolific writer. His magnum opus (in my opinion), Re-visioning Psychology, was written in 1975 and nominated for the Pulitzer Prize. He is also an international lecturer and a private practitioner in Jungian analysis.

The Soul's Code was on the New York Time's best seller list. Though it's a difficult read, once I plowed through it, I came out of it with a knowledge about myself and my 30 years of addiction that I probably would have gone my entire life without realizing. This knowledge was gleaned from his *acorn theory*, which proposes that each life is formed by a particular image (which he calls the daimon), an image that is the essence of that life and calls it to a destiny, just as the mighty oak's destiny is written in the tiny acorn. Therefore, I believe that my first life of addiction was preordained by the acorn theory, so that I could do what I've done in my second life.

141

Chapter Thirteen References

Adler, A. (1964). *Social interest: A challenge to mankind*. New York: Capricorn.

Allport, G. (1954). *The nature of prejudice*. Reading, Massachusetts: Addison-Wesley.

Cohen, D. (1977). *Psychologists on psychology*. New York: Taplinger.

Dollard, J. (1937). *Caste and class in a southern town*. Madison, Wisconsin: University of Wisconsin.

Ewen, R. (1988). *Theories of personality*. Hillsdale, N.J.: Lawrence Erlbaum.

Ferris, P. (1997. *Dr. Freud: A life*. Washington, DC: Counterpoint.

Freud, S. (1961). *The future of an illusion*. New York: W.W. Norton & Company.

Fromm, E. (1976). *To have or to be*. New York: Harper & Row.

Goble, F. (1970). *The third force: The psychology of Abraham Maslow*. New York: Grossman:

Hillman, J. (1975). *Re-visioning psychology*. New York: HarperPerennial.

Hillman, J. (1996). *The soul's code*. New York: Random House.

Horney, K (1967). *Feminine psychology*. New York: W.W. Norton.

Jung, C. (1953). "Two essays on analytical psychology." In R. F. C. Hull (Trans.), The collected works of C. G. Jung (Vol. 7). New York: Pantheon Books, Inc. (Original works published in 1943, 1945).

Jung, C.. (1953). *Psychological reflections*. New York: Harper and Row. p. 120.

Lundin, R. (1991).*Theories and systems of psychology*. Lexington, Massachusetts: D.C. Heath.

May, R (1967). *Psychology and the human dilemma*. New York: W. W. Norton.

Nakken, C. (1988). *The addictive personality*. San Francisco: Harper & Row.

Roazen, P. (1976). *The power and limits of a vision*. London: Collier Macmillan.

Rogers, C. (1970). *Carl Rogers on encounter groups*. New York: Harper & Row.

Skinner, B. F. (1974). *About behaviorism*. New York: Alfred A. Knopf.

CHAPTER FOURTEEN

Psychopathy

The difference between a psychopath and a sociopath is blurred, at least according to the Diagnostic and Statistical Manual of Mental Disorders (DSM). The DSM lists both definitions together under the heading of Antisocial Personalities because they share common traits. However, some professionals maintain that there is a difference beyond the similarities. Henceforth, I'll use the terms psychopathy and psychopath rather than the alternative.

Psychopathy consists of a group of personality traits and behaviors, which includes irresponsibility, impulsivity, hedonism, selfishness, egocentricity, low frustration tolerance, lack of guilt, remorse or shame. Psychopaths are selfish, callous, and exploitative in their use of others, and often become involved in socially deviant behaviors. These traits and behaviors appear in psychopaths without the signs of psychosis, neurosis, or mental deficiency found in most other mental illnesses. Psychopaths make up approximately 15 to 20 percent of criminal populations but are responsible for more crimes and violent acts.

In comparison addicts are also irresponsible, impulsive, hedonistic, selfish, egocentric, and have a low frustration tolerance. Unlike psychopaths, they're not without guilt, remorse or shame, which is the major difference between the two. Addicts are also selfish, sometimes callous, and often exploitative in their use of others, and depending on their drug of choice, will participate in socially deviant behaviors. Addicts make up approximately 70 percent of criminal populations and are responsible for more crimes and violent acts than even psychopaths.

The personality structure and life history of the psychopath are quite different from those whose antisocial or criminal behavior is related to an emotional disturbance, and from those of a person whose antisocial behavior results from living in a criminal subculture or in an environment in which such behavior is expected or rewarded, such as the criminal behavior resulting from chemical dependency. Unlike the psychopath, these individuals may be capable of forming strong affectionate relationships and of experiencing concern and guilt over their behavior.

Having been chemically dependent for so many years of my life, I was therefore engaged in criminal activity of various kinds. For example, for ten years I obtained controlled substances by writing and calling in my own medical prescriptions. To read about my scrip-running exploits, go to my website at www.ScumbagSewerRats.com, and click on my article Prescription for addiction. For about 13 years I was also employed in service stations defrauding the public by selling tires, shocks, fan clutches, and fuel pumps, and I did this by highly unethical, not to mention illegal, sales practices. There's also an article on my website about that, entitled Lube Bay Bandits. Of course, I indulged in other kinds of illegal activity because of my chemical needs, but that's not the focus of this paper.

"The criminal [psychopath] approaches the world with a sense of ownership," says Samenow, (1989),

> ..as though people and objects are mere pawns on his personal chessboard. He aims to control other people just to enhance his own sense of power. Human relationships are avenues through which he pursues conquests and triumphs. The criminal expects others to do whatever he wants without hesitation. He delights in arguing for the sake of arguing. He is intent on winning what he regards as a battle, no matter how trivial the issue. This type of individual is a master at ferreting out weaknesses in others and ruthlessly taking advantage of them. When people oppose him, he can be merciless. Nearly everything he does, he does to feel powerful (pp. 14, 15).

The 'criminal' in the previous paragraph can be either psychopathic or, like me, one of those whose criminal activity is exacerbated by the illicit use of drugs. Obviously, there's not a fine line that demarcates which behaviors are relegated to psychopathy, and which are relegated to addiction. There's overlap, and much of it depends on the individual. There are addicts who have elements of psychopathy, and of course there are a great many psychopaths who are chemically dependent.

Psychopaths are usually loners. Although they associate with people they *call* friends, no one ever really knows them. They are pathological liars; however, even the lies that are seemingly senseless makes sense when one understands their motives. When they believe they are getting over on someone, they feel that they have the edge. Every time they get away with something, they find it exciting. These attributes aren't as fixed in addicts as much as they are in psychopaths. So much depends on the duration of addiction, drugs of choice, and personal history, not to mention their socioeconomic and cultural backgrounds.

Psychopaths take from others, but rarely give anything without an ulterior motive. These people don't know what trust, love, or loyalty is. If they can gain something for themselves, they will betray their best friend. These people are so focused on pursuing their immediate objectives that they don't care what others think, nor do they consider their feelings. Invariably, they hurt those who care about them most. In one way or another, mothers, fathers, siblings, spouses, and children of psychopath's all become his victims with no feeling of remorse.

A majority of the chemically dependent, who employ some of the above behaviors, do target their families, but at least most of them will have remorse. This remorse usually ends up on a fourth step if they ever make it into the recovery process.

Herrnstein and Wilson (1985) emphasize that;

> To a criminal [psychopath], life consists of a series of essentially unrelated events in which he seeks immediate gain and a buildup. He plots and connives, but rarely plans. With a winning personality, the criminal gains the trust and confidence of others and then preys upon them. Even the most cold-blooded criminal regards himself as a decent person. A man who had killed two police officers commented with complete sincerity that just because he murdered a couple of people, he was not a bad person (p. 218, 219).

"Conventional wisdom," McGuire (1993) reminds us, "claims that if a youngster has serious problems, the parents must be the source. This point of view was prevalent for decades. Some children at a preschool age have characteristics that predict later crime " (p.12).

Preschool aged children also have characteristics that predict chemical dependency, but they aren't as easy to identify because those same characteristics also predict crime and other types of antisocial behavior. It's also well established that if a child is raised by alcoholic or drug-addicted parents, then those parents are the source of their youngster's problems with addictive substances later in life. If the parents aren't substance abusers, and the youngster turns to drugs and/or alcohol later in life, then the source for that dependency, and the characteristics that predict it, aren't as easy to identify.

Wilson (1992) talks about conventional wisdom when he stated that;

> We thought we knew all the answers: Children are wholly the products of their parents. We now know that the child brings a great deal to the parent-child relationship. Many aspects of personality have genetic origins, and some infants experience insults and traumas - ranging from lead poisoning to brain injuries - that makes rearing them a challenge to even the most competent parents. Two children in the same family often turn out differently. This casts great doubt on the notion that the shared environment of the children is the principle - or even an important factor in their development (p. A 40).

Another form of infantile trauma that isn't discussed much is birth trauma. For example, when I was borne, the attending physician used forceps to pull me out of the womb. Upon entering the world, my mother and I were both dead for over a minute - at least our hearts stopped beating for that long. The team managed to resuscitate us. I was left with part of my head being crushed in from the use of the forceps. Could the trauma I experienced at birth have predisposed me to chemical dependency later in life? Who can say? My mother was a periodic alcoholic, and I had a couple of visiting uncles who were alcoholics too, so causes, especially when it comes to addiction, are wide and varied and hard to determine on an individual basis.

"The daily experiences," as Samenow (1989) points out,

146

..of millions of parents, as well as a body of psychological research, suggest that the child is not a passive receptacle. Rather than haplessly being shaped by his surroundings, he himself shapes the behavior of others. Two researchers in the field of child development have pointed out that any credible model of child development must consider the child as an active agent in social transactions. Any parent of more than one child knows that children differ in temperament from birth. One infant may be fussy, irritable, and restless; another may be placid and contented. Isn't it natural for a parent to respond differently to a cranky, colicky baby than to a cooing, quiet one? Whereas most parents 'try' to raise their children with love and to provide them equally with opportunities, they invariably treat each differently. It could not be otherwise for, from birth, children have different temperaments, personalities, and needs (p. 29, 30).

What does this have to do with crime? Quite a bit, as far as identifying the source of the problem. If one were a fly on the wall in the office of a psychologist, one would hear juvenile offenders blame their parents, and parents blame themselves for their youngsters' misconduct. Many of these boys and girls who realize just how vulnerable their parents are to feelings of guilt, will level increasingly serious accusations against them. And so mothers and fathers who already doubt themselves as parents become even more guilt-ridden, depressed, and often angry with each other.

Take early school experiences, for example. Poor performance in school is one of the strongest correlates of misconduct; however, what explains school performance? One possibility is that teachers label some children as troublemakers and slow learners and treat them in ways that becomes a self-fulfilling prophecy because they internalize what they're being told. Another is that children with low IQs find school work boring and frustrating and turn to physical activity, such as acting out in the classroom. This also can apply to those with considerably high IQs.

The DSM, as I mentioned at the beginning of this paper, is the standard reference for establishing diagnostic criteria for mental disorders. It flatly states that the diagnosis of antisocial personality disorder (psychopathy) must not be applied to anyone under the age of eighteen; furthermore, the DSM will only categorize an adult over 18 as an antisocial personality. Instead, the term "conduct disorder" applies to children. It takes time for personalities to gel, and it is important not to mislabel a juvenile in a manner that might be harmful. The DSM doesn't state anything about age concerning substance-related disorders. Nowadays children are drinking and using drugs at younger ages, and it is not uncommon for parents to *turn their kids on* to alcohol and/or drugs.

There are pros and cons concerning psychiatric labels, but their use often conceals far more than they reveal and are open to misinterpretation. However, what is important is how a child is functioning - how he or she behaves and perceives themselves and the world.

"As often happens with many personality disorders," says Carson and Butcher (1992),

> The causal factors in antisocial personality are still not fully understood. The perspective is complicated by the fact that the causal factors involved appear to differ from case to case, also from one socioeconomic level to another. Contemporary research in this area has variously stressed the causal roles of constitutional deficiencies, the early learning of antisocial behavior as a coping style, and the influence of particular family and community patterns (pp. 286-289).

The causal factors in substance-related disorders are not fully understood either, and the reasons are consistent with those in the preceding paragraph. Also, the problem with chemical dependency is further complicated by so many conflicting theories such as the nature/nurture controversy.

Biological factors
Because a psychopath's impulsiveness, acting out, and intolerance of discipline tends to appear early in life, several investigators have focused on the role of biological factors as causative agents. Research

evidence indicates that a primary reaction tendency typically found in psychopaths is a deficient emotional arousal; this condition presumably renders them less prone to fear and anxiety in stressful situations and less prone to normal conscience development and socialization.

Behaviors that lead to the taking of drugs are gradually strengthened through operant and classical conditioning processes and by biochemical changes in the brain. What do we do when we do something we like? We do it again. We like the way drugs make us feel, so we want to do it again.

Stimulation Seeking

In a study of psychopaths, it was reported that they operate at low levels of arousal and are deficient in autonomic variability. These characteristics suggest a relative immunity to stimulation, which would likely prompt them to seek stimulations and thrill as ends in themselves.

There are those who contend that altering consciousness is innate. Chemical substances certainly alter consciousness. However, perhaps the internal needs to release inhibitions, be devious, act crazy, fight, gamble, lie, cheat, steal, and pursue recreational sex, is also an innate need to alter consciousness. Endorphins, a chemical substance produced by the brain, also alters consciousness, hence the runners high.

Genetic Influence

This sociobiological theory assumes a genetic influence on predispositions for particular behaviors. The validity of this view point is not conclusive. However, it provides some interesting leads for researchers to follow in further studies. Perhaps the most popular generalization about the development of psychopathy is the assumption of some form of early disturbance in family relationships.

The nature side of the nature/nurture controversy contends that alcoholism is genetic, or that addiction is genetic. Whereas I don't support that theory, it's more likely that a predisposition to an addictive personality is genetic, rather than an addictive predisposition to a specific substance such as alcohol. Therefore, the controversial gene is more likely to manifest in any number of addictive behaviors, such as sex addiction, overeating, gambling, shopping, etc.

Parental Rejection and Inconsistency

Two types of parental behavior foster psychopathy. In the first, parents are cold and distant toward a child and do not allow a warm or close relationship to develop. A child who imitates this parental model will become cold and distant in later relationships. The second type involves inconsistency, in which parents are capricious in supplying affection, rewards, and punishments. Usually they are inconsistent in their own role enactments as well, so that a child lacks stable models to imitate and fails to develop a clear-cut sense of self-identity. When parents are both arbitrary and inconsistent in punishing a child, avoiding punishment becomes more important than receiving rewards. Instead of learning to see behavior in terms or right and wrong, the child learns how to avoid blame and punishment by lying or other manipulative means.

If parental rejection and inconsistency are so prevalent with psychopaths, then how could it not be so with the chemically dependent, at least to some degree? Perhaps the severity of this neglect is a determining factor.

Sociocultural Factors

Psychopathy is thought to be more common in lower socioeconomic groups. Although constitutional and family factors have been emphasized, it appears that social conditions such as those found in our urban ghettos also produce their share of psychopaths.

This is also consistent in drug and alcohol studies over the years, but there's considerably more addicts, especially alcoholics, in the higher socioeconomic groups - at least more so than with psychopaths.

What I've presented here is not comprehensive. It's just a brief overview. Furthermore, the human condition and overall knowledge of the brain and how it works is in its infancy. Perhaps some people are destined to live by principles that we are unaware of. Perhaps there is far more than we would like to admit that we simply don't know. Perhaps many of our present theories are wrong.

Chapter Fourteen References

Carson, Robert C., and Butcher, James N. (1992). *Abnormal psychology and modern life*. New York: Harper Collins.

Herrnstein, Richard J., and Wilson, James Q. (1985). *Crime and human nature*. New York: Simon and Schuster.

McGuire, Jacqueline. (July/August 1993). "Primed for crime." *Psychology Today*.

Samenow, Stanton E. (1989). *Before it's too late*. New York: Times Books.

Wilson, James Q. (June 10, 1992). "Scholars must expand our understanding of criminal behavior." *The Chronicle of Higher Education*.

CHAPTER FIFTEEN

DUI

This short paper and the following one aren't coming from the perspective of depth psychology like the subtitle of this book indicates; however, it's hard to deny that drunk driving is a part of the *shadow* side of the human condition. Not all archetypes are personified in all people, but the shadow is. There's a dark side to everybody's personality.

To list the many reasons to abstain from driving while under the influence of drugs and/or alcohol (DUI) would fill a book. I believe, however, there is a need for devising new strategies in an attempt to curtail the high incidence of DUI, and in the process, lower the high mortality and injury rates because of it. Throughout the United States, variations of paying fines, temporary loss of driver license, DUI school, and increased insurance rates is a slap on the hand for a first offense. Let's examine each of these individually:

Fines
Paying a fine, regardless of how much it is, doesn't curtail the behavior at all. The courts allow offenders to make payments, just like a department store or any credit-giving institution. The conviction, even though DUI is a misdemeanor, is still a conviction - the convicts will incorporate installments like they do their car or house payments, or anything else they buy on credit. It simply becomes another bill. By no means am I suggesting that we eliminate fines, if anything, we should increase them considerably. Why should we raise the fines if it doesn't curtail the behavior? Because we would be doing it, not for punishment, but for restitution.

Not every DUI involves injury to others, the loss of lives, or the destruction of personal property. However, expecting convicts who have deprived others, can't be expected to compensate the victims alone, so it should be disseminated. This is already being done in many states, but not to the degree that I'm suggesting.

According to MADD (mothers against drunk drivers), first offense fines across the United States range from $200. to $1,000. I suggest imposing a fine of $10,000.00 for the first offense, and spread the payment plan over a period of years. Part of the proceeds could also be allotted to recovery programs, DUI schools, drug courts, victim restitution programs, and other benevolent institutions and societies who'd be willing to administer to victims of DUI.

Loss of Drivers License
This is probably the most debilitating. People need to get to work, so they can make the money that's necessary to live on, and of course to pay the fines. I don't need to itemize all the reasons why we need transportation. However, if DUI is going to be discouraged, we need to stop slapping their hands. In the United States, driver license suspension for a first offense ranges from ten days to six months - the average is three to four months. During that time they get used to it. They incorporate into their lives a way to get by without driving. Either that, or they drive anyway, which isn't uncommon. Many even continue to drink and drive. In 1984, I was arrested on a DUI charge while I was going to court for a DUI charge. I still didn't stop drinking and driving, and I wasn't unique.

Why not revoke their license for five years? If they can get used to a suspension for three to four months, they can get used to it for five years. However, it's doubtful that they could get away with continuing driving for that long without getting caught. With first offenses being so devastating by the loss of their license for that long, the incidence of repeat offenders would be considerably decreased. In addition to license revocation, their vehicle should also be confiscated, auctioned off, and the proceeds divided between recovery programs, DUI schools, drug courts, victim restitution programs, and various benevolent institutions and societies who'd be willing to administer to victims of DUI.

DUI School
For a first offense, in California for example, the DUI offender must attend nine weeks of DUI school. A second offense is increased to a year. It was my observation as a counselor in a DUI school, that most

offenders resist the education provided to them because they view their forced attendance as punishment. They resent being there so they put up walls to block information that cold save their own lives and the lives of others. By spreading the required attendance to five years for a first offense, it's possible that the extensive education would eventually start sinking in, maybe taking as long as a couple of years. Forced education often works. Having attended 12-step meetings for more than 15 years, I witnessed many newcomers resisting everything that was being said at meetings. I have also witnessed several of those newcomers achieving lasting and intrinsic recovery. Many of those members were forced into meetings by the courts, child protective services, employers, and spouses. It was either stop drinking or suffer the consequences. The extrinsic reasons for attendance often turn into intrinsic reasons after varying amounts of time. Many of them also come and go, and then some finally stay. Then others never come back. With mandatory DUI school for five years, there is plenty of time for the counselors to convert their clients' resistence to a willingness to learn and accept and then be able to apply the information that is being offered.

Insurance

Insurance companies set the rates for insurance. Most people may be surprised to learn that when an insurer does find out about a DUI conviction, the company doesn't automatically impose higher premiums. The insurer will look at the insured's history with the company and their claims record. For example, State Farm's action depends on which subsidiary within the company the insured is with. If they have a preferred policy with State Farm Mutual Insurance Company. and receive a DUI, State Farm has the option move them into State Farm Fire & Casualty, which is a standard-policy company. If moved from preferred to a standard status, they'll be paying higher rates already. State Farm will also review their motor vehicle and insurance claims history to determine if it needs to raise the rates even more.

South Carolina has 'integrated' insurance laws wherein all convictions *must* be reported to insurance carriers and the rates paid *must* be increased by the carriers, in accordance with a legislated formula designed to penalize high risk drivers. Something similar could be done in California, or better yet, nation wide.

Conclusion

Are fines, loss of driver license, DUI school, and increased insurance rates enough to deter DUI offenders? Possibly, for some offenders, of course, but there are those who won't stop until they are dead. Let's look at what happens to first offenders in other countries. In Guam they serve a minimum of 48 hours of imprisonment, a mandatory fine of $1,000.00 not to exceed $5,000.00, and a six-month loss of their driving privilege. This information came from the following website: http://www.lawyernet.com/members/jimfesq/DDD.html (now defunct).

In Pakistan drinking alcohol is illegal. In Hong Kong if driving under the influence beyond the legal limit, one can be fined and jailed up to three years. Found at:
http://en.wikipedia.org/wiki/Driving_under_the_influence

Germany has increased its drunken-driving penalties and now people with a blood alcohol level of .05 or more caught operating a vehicle will have their licenses suspended for a month. Furthermore, if the BAC is between .05 and .079, license is suspended for 90 days, between .08 and .099 license is suspended for 180 days, for a BAC level of .1 and above, license can be suspended indefinitely. Found at: http://ww2.pstripes.osd.mil/01/apr01/ed040301e.html (now defunct).

Belgium has strict drunk-driving laws, only allowing 0.25mg/ml of alcohol in the blood. Fines range from 125 on-the-spot to 2,500 (if prosecuted) and up to a maximum of 10,000 (if over 0.8mg/l), a six-month sentence and five-year suspension of driver licence. Found at http://www.shareyourstate.com/worldtravel/belgiumdriving.htm (now defunct).

The following was retrieved from:
http://en.wikipedia.org/wiki/Drunk_driving_law_by_country, which includes additional countries.

East Asia:
China: 0.02% (CNY 200–500 fine, 1–17 months license suspension); 0.78% (up to 15 days prison, 3 years licence suspension, CNY 500-2000 fine). Beginning May 1, 2011, Chinese law now mandates a penal detention up to 6 months for any person convicted of drunken driving.

(In China, penal detention is a criminal punishment similar to, but less severe than prison.

Hong Kong: 0.05% or BrAC 0.22 mg/L or urine 0.067%. Driving under the influence of alcohol beyond legal limit is punishable with a monetary fine and up to three years imprisonment, with 10 driving-offense points and mandatory Driving Improvement Course.

Japan: BrAC 0.15 mg/L (equivalent to 0.03%). Additionally, regardless of alcohol readings, police may also determine the driver to be "driving drunk," which is punished more severely than exceeding the designated alcohol limits.

Taiwan: Over 0.05% but under 0.11%: TWD 15,000 to 90,000 fine, and license suspension for 1 year. 0.11% and above: license suspension for 1 year, and charge of offences against public safety with possible prison sentence up to 2 years as the maximum penalty. If the driver is convicted of causing accidents, the penalty shall be increased by half. If the driver causes serious injuries or death, the license will be suspended for life.

As you can see, the laws in other countries vary. Obviously, there is not a high incidence of DUI in countries with the harshest laws; therefore, it seems only logical that penalties are such that they actually deter driving under the influence. A slap on the hand is not a deterrent.

CHAPTER SIXTEEN

Prison Doesn't Work

(As published in the 1995 issue of Pleiades Magazine)

I heard the correction officer's keys jingling before he unlocked the dorm door. I walked down the sidewalk toward the yard and heard all the voices. When I approached the yard, I saw a huge day-care center before me. The sun was shining, and there was a cool breeze. There were Mansons and Dahmers everywhere. Some were playing soccer, some basketball, and others were throwing frisbees. They were working out on the weight pile, playing cards on picnic tables, and many were just walking around the yard talking with their friends. The tennis and handball courts were also occupied. Others were cheering their favorite team in the bleachers while watching the softball game. After looking around for a while, I was amazed that I couldn't find one inmate that looked unhappy or depressed. That suggested to me that prison doesn't work in the capacity that it was designed for.

The federal, and most of the state prison systems are huge day-care centers or kindergartens. Prison is not a deterrent to crime. Education is, however. By using myself as an example, I'll show how education worked for me, and how it could work for countless others.

While I was a ward of the California Department of Corrections (CDC), I found that much of the inmate population didn't really mind being there. There are those who'd say that they were institutionalized, and maybe some of them were, but not all of them. Quoted in previous paper from my magazine article, I explained that;

> *"inmates are well provided for, having little, if no responsibility for themselves. Our clothes and linen were cleaned for us every week - all we had to do is drop it off and pick it up; our meals were provided for us - all we had to do is show up, wait in line, and eat. We had a big yard to play on - a weight pile where we could flex our muscles, show off, and be macho, then strut around the yard acting tough (many of them really are), much like kids do on the*

playground. We build reputations, status, and respect from our peers by controlling the drug and alcohol flow, managing moneymaking schemes, and having our subordinates do our dirty work. Drugs are plentiful on the yard, and pruno (home-made wine) is easily made. Every three months we can have money and material things (a package) sent to us from outside the walls. If we are married, we can even spend a weekend in a bungalow with our wives and relieve ourselves sexually. In prisons that have rooms (cells), we can enjoy watching our own TV."

No, the prison system doesn't work.

Amazing! It seems to me, we are encouraging crime, not preventing it, by building miniature cities (prisons) for criminals to rule their prospective kingdoms. They have it made. I was there and this is what I observed. I asked Rick, a man doing three years for several consecutive drunk drivings, "Do you really want to get out? I get the impression you like it here." His reply was, "of course I do, home boy, I can't wait to hit the streets."

He believed what he said; however, I believe he had an unconscious want and/or need to stay where he was. To prove it, when he's released he'll not make a single attempt to reform his life. He'll commit crimes and/or take drugs with no worry of getting caught. Why worry? If he gets caught, some judge will just send him back home. Prison just doesn't work.

I can't count the times I was in county jail and had conversations much like this: "Have you gone to court yet, bro?"

"Tomorrow, homeboy, then it's back to the joint."

"You sound like you want to go there."

"Shit homes, I'd rather do a year in the joint than thirty days in this hole." That is the typical attitude of prisoners in the county jail waiting for sentencing, and I agree 100%, for county jail is hell compared to the comforts of the California state or federal prison systems. I can't speak about prisons in the rest of the states

Recidivism is high; the typical inmate will be back in the joint on a violation usually within months, and then the revolving door process continues. Jack, a buddy I grew up with began his addiction to heroin when he was around 22 years old. Before this, he'd served several county jail sentences that were alcohol related. Because of armed robberies, burglaries, petty and grand thefts, under the influence charges, and other drug related offenses, he has spent most of his life in prison. Not once did he ever take the first step toward rehabilitation. He wouldn't admit that he didn't mind being in prison, but what was his behavior saying? Prison wasn't the least bit of a threat to him. Jack is doing life now. A high-speed chase ended in a head-on collision. He had just pulled an armed robbery. He got the third strike three times for three felonies, and an additional five years.

Consciously, most of us think we don't want to get caught, but unconsciously our behavior is saying, "Catch me, so I can go back home, where I will be taken care of and provided for." How is a person on the inside made to prepare for a law-abiding life on the outside? In no way really. By taking away responsibility by being placed in the prison system, the inmate becomes less responsible. His self-reliance is atrophied. There is no understanding or no rehabilitation. We inmates were provided with jobs, so we can earn money, for not all of us are lucky enough to have family sending us packages every three months. However, how does that teach us responsibility when our only other option is lock up if we refuse to work? Here is a conversation I had with one of my bunkies when I was in the Chino Guiding Center:

"What are you going to do when you get out, Solidad?"

"Get high, Dude. First thing."

"Aren't you afraid of getting violated and sent back?"

"Yeah, but the P.O. [parole officer] isn't going to test me on my first day out."

Solidad doesn't plan on returning to prison on a violation, but with his attitude, he doesn't stand a chance of being successfully discharged from parole. Furthermore, he isn't really worried about whether he returns to prison or not; because prison really doesn't work.

One evening I was standing in line for commissary, and I overheard a conversation going on between two inmates in front of me: "You know, homey, I wouldn't be here for robbin' that liquor store if the damn clutch wasn't bad in that old Chevy of mine. Just as I was taking off, the motor died. I got it started, then it died again. That happened three times. By the time I made it to the corner there were red lights everywhere."

At the time I could identify, because I have all too often placed the blame for my behavior outside of me. It would have been a waste of time for me to say, "hey man, you wouldn't be here for robbin a liquor store if you hadn't been robbing a liquor store." It's strange, but that obvious statement doesn't seem to occur to them. It wouldn't have to me either. When I was a bartender, I was in the bar on my night off. A couple guys asked if I could get them some drugs. I said no. Later they asked me again. And again I said no. However, when they asked me again around one o'clock in the morning I knew there was some in the bar, so I got it for them. They were under cover policemen. I fought it in a jury trial and lost. I appealed it, and lost that too. I was entrapped! It wasn't my fault! They were picking on me! The truth is, if I wouldn't have been selling drugs, I wouldn't have gone to prison for selling drugs. However, I was not capable of seeing it that way.

Most inmates don't want anything to do with the responsibility of living in the outside world. William Glasser, author of *Reality Therapy*, wrote about it: "He broke the law not because he was angry or bored, but because he was irresponsible. The unhappiness is not a cause but a companion to his irresponsible behavior." The streets are a frightening place to be, because being responsible and accountable for their actions is alien to them. The whole idea of prison for punishment is backwards.

Most of us go to prison because of, directly or indirectly, drugs and/or alcohol. I was a practicing alcoholic and drug addict for more than thirty years, and finally my addiction took me to the penitentiary. I was lucky though; the facility where I was last incarcerated started a treatment program for substance abusers, and I got in on it. Judging from my experience, if the inmates with chemical dependency problems

160

can be educated about their disease, they can learn that they have a choice other than prison, insanity, or death. They could be provided with tools that might lead them to a happy and productive life on the streets. I knew nothing other than dependence on chemicals for all those years.

What follows is found in chapter one, so unless readers don't mind reading it again, the section that follows in *italics* can be skipped.

After I left the Chino Guiding Center, I was transferred to Sierra Conservation Center at Jamestown, California. It was there that I encountered Project Change - a substance abuse education program. We lived in dorms that housed thirty-three people (designed for twenty-two), and every day teachers from the education department came to our dorm. We held classes in the television room. Our teachers were dedicated. Mary, the one that did most of the work putting the program together, is often in my thoughts. She talked about her drug addict brother, and admitted to some drug and alcohol use when she was younger; therefore, we felt that she had more than just a job to do. She had a personal interest, which was more than just another academic endeavor. Had it not been for her, I probably wouldn't have a Ph.D. today. She convinced me that I was capable of success if I went back to school. Before my release, she helped me fill out all the tedious financial aide forms, and I mailed them to Barstow College from there. When I got out, all I had to do was enroll. Sixty days after I left prison, I was sitting in college classrooms, and I did that for 12 years.

In Project Change we were taught about dysfunctional families, 12-step programs, relapse prevention, anger control, health, depression, family unity, family violence, co-dependency, and much more. The program was voluntary, and the inmates that participated really got involved. One of the most inspirational and motivating segments of the program for me, was a series of video tapes orated by Gordon Graham called Breaking Barriers. These tapes taught me that 'change' was the way out of the mental prison that I had been confined in for so many years. I learned that I had to monitor and discipline my thoughts. When I had thoughts of going to the places where I previously drank and used drugs, I had to stop thinking about that and start thinking about something else. Before I was sent to the pen, I worked in a biker bar as a bartender where I had an unlimited amount of alcohol at my disposal. I partied there a lot too, spending time there when I wasn't working. When I wasn't there, I was going to the connection's house and buying drugs, or to friends' house selling them. I thought of all the people I associated with, especially the women. Thinking about all of that had to stop. Creating imagery of where I wanted to be when I was released was imperative to my recovery. Cognitive therapy calls this process 'thought stopping.' In my mind's eye, I pictured myself in AA meetings and in college classrooms. It took a long time for me to keep those negative thoughts from entering my mind. When they would come, I would shoo them away. Sometimes it took awhile before I realized that I was thinking them, but as I kept exorcizing the recurring thoughts, and replacing them with the ones of where I really wanted to be, eventually they didn't come anymore. Because of this painstaking mental exercise, everything that I forced myself to think about while I was incarcerated, has come true today. Before Project Change I had no intentions of ever quitting drugs and/or alcohol - for I thought that was what I wanted to do indefinitely. My thinking was, Why change? What's the use?

Change is the key to rehabilitation, and the key to change is education. In my case, the education I received in Project Change was what initiated my recovery. For true change, real change, it has to come from within. Education is the only way this can be accomplished.

For a long time it has been believed that prison is punishment. Judges still send people to prison for punishment. In truth, prison simply doesn't work. As I walked around the yard, I could see the comfort zone that most of the inmates were in - they were relaxed and at home. Their jovial camaraderie, "Hey, home-boy, what it be like?" would give anyone the impression that they were in their element. The human condition can get used to most anything, and it is all too visible there. They are used to doing time. When I see those types of people on the street, they don't have the appearance of being in a comfort zone - that relaxed, at home appearance. They seem more on edge, even thought it's subtle. For good reason, they have much more to be on edge about. Everything isn't handed to them the way it is in the joint. The appreciation of freedom is a sophisticated concept. It involves the appreciation of others (healthy relationships), interaction (socialization), helping others (without expecting anything in return), and mutual caring (love). Prison types that I see on the street don't have these qualities because they haven't been taught how.

Project Change was a spiritual or psychological experience for me, because finally I knew that I was mentally sober - not just abstinent. Before Project Change, I held everything outside me at fault; there was no real me; my life was controlled by my surroundings - whether I was on the streets or in jail. I was unproductive to my environment. After I was released, I began to think of others instead of just myself; I attended 12-step meetings where I started learning social skills and how to help others; I learned to accept my fellow human beings whether I liked them or not. I started seeing that I could create my own world and live happy. If this *inside* change didn't occur, I would have returned to the only lifestyle I'd ever known - alcohol, drugs, and then eventually back to prison where life is like a day care center.

So, the government, due to popular misconceptions about prisons and what they are for, keeps spending money to put more people in them. Toward what end? To make crime more attractive? No, prison doesn't work.

A similar phenomenon occurred in the mental health field several years ago called The Hospitalization Syndrome. Many who resided in large mental hospitals over long periods of time tended to adopt a passive role, losing the self-confidence and motivation required for reentering the outside world. They were saddled with what's referred to as deficiency in self-concept. In institutions that served primarily as "storage bins" for the emotionally disturbed, basic work and social skills would atrophy through disuse. The same goes for prisons. They are also storage bins. There's no boubt a doubt it - prison does not work.

Twenty years previous to the time I wrote this article, California started planning both operating budgets for prisons and construction costs at levels far more than those that funded the entire prison system of the United States 20 years previous to that. Then again, the state anticipated having a larger prison population by the end of that decade - more than that of all 50 states in 1973. For 20 years henceforth, as the number of prisoners doubled and then tripled in the United States, the policies behind prison expansion had been unexamined as well as uncontested. I was released from CDC in December 1989. Then, both of the institutions where I was confined were extremely overcrowded. The prison population is even more overcrowded now. As of November 1994, in California, the prison population reached one million. Obviously, prison doesn't work.

CHAPTER SEVENTEEN

Quantum Phenomenology

According to Goswami (1995) "whenever we ask if there is some other kind of reality beyond material reality, we are putting material realism on the spot. Similarly, a genuine discontinuity points to a transcendent order of reality and thus a breakdown of material realism" (p. 138). What follows wrote itself. I didn't have much to do with it. What started as an idea in a classroom environment must have continued developing without my being aware of it. Perhaps a dream contributed to its development, I don't know. Furthermore, quantum recovery is probably a better description of what follows than quantum physics/mechanics, but I landed on phenomenology because I see it as phenomenal. Though this does suggest a transcendent order of reality, it doesn't necessarily point to a breakdown of material realism.

I got off work at six o'clock in the evening, went home and sifted through my mail, listened to my phone messages, then went to a restaurant for dinner. As I was waiting in line to pay my bill, the man in front of me turned around to leave and we made eye contact. "Wow, is that really you?" We had not seen each other in 25 years. We stepped outside, and after a few minutes of small talk, he asked if I wanted to hang out for a while and catch up. I said yes. He told me that he was supposed to meet someone at a local bar, and his business would only take a short while. Considering how long I'd been clean and sober, I didn't think it would be too risky to go with him and chat for a while. *Nuncest bibendum* - now is the time to drink. Three hours later, after ten years clean and sober, we were still in the bar and I was well on my way to getting drunk. We also did some drugs together like we did so many years before. On the way to my house to sleep it off, the police pulled us over - the last thing I remember was being fingerprinted.

I then woke up in a cold sweat and in a state of panic. "Did that really happen?" I asked myself.

Yes, it did happen. I met Jon in the restaurant one day, but we went our separate ways after exchanging phone numbers and a few minutes of small talk outside of the restaurant. Maybe he went to the bar. I don't know. I went back home, however, and resumed working on a paper I started a couple nights earlier. So, how could it have happened if I went home? Folger (September, 2001) quotes Deutsch as saying that "we have every possible option we've ever encountered acted out somewhere in some universe by at least one of our other selves" (p. 39). In theoretical physics, this theory–which there has been several books written about–is the quantum view of parallel universes.

Without going into how Deutsch and other physicists arrive at this conclusion, I will say that, like a particle in quantum mechanics, we too can be in more than one place at a time. "Under normal circumstances," says Deutsch, "we never encounter the multiple realities of quantum mechanics. We certainly aren't aware of what our other selves are doing" (p. 40). Well, maybe we aren't, but maybe we are. Was I not dreaming about drinking and using with Jon? Why couldn't the dream be an awareness of one of my other selves? So which is it? Is it two me's in parallel universes, or one me having a dream? Maybe it's both. Perhaps it's what Freud considered a wish fulfillment, or maybe the dream was having me - rather than the other way around. Maybe I was observing my other universe through a dream. Let's put these maybes on hold for now and come back to them later.

There are people who remember me as a disgraceful drug addict from as far back as the mid sixties. Over the years prior to recovery, through reputation, their image of me has been reinforced by my scandalous behavior. This also goes for my old friend, Jon, for he too has been a hedonistic, immutable career drug addict. I have no reason to believe that he is any different today than he was when we ran together years ago. When Jon and I were talking outside of the restaurant, I told him that I'd been clean and sober for twelve years and I've earned a Ph.D. He looked at me quizzically, smiled and said, "yeah, right."

Goswami (1995) tells the story

> about a student who taught a frog to jump: Frog, jump, and the frog jumped. The student cut off one of the frog's legs and said: frog, jump, and the frog jumped. He cut off a second leg: frog,

jump, and the frog jumped. The same thing happened after cutting off the third leg. When the student cut off the last leg, the frog did not jump. After a moment's thought, the student wrote: After losing all four legs, the frog loses its hearing (p. 219).

The same goes with Jon's thinking when it concerns me. If I'd shown him my doctoral degree, he would've asked "that's nice, who printed it for you?" If I'd introduced him to one of my professors, he would've considered it a conspiracy. If I'd shown him my transcripts, he would have shrugged and said "computer generated, so what?" Jon would have to personally observe me for quite awhile before he would be convinced that my recovery, much less my level of education, existed. I find the frog parable synonymous to the quantum object that doesn't exist until it is observed.

A quantum particle doesn't exist until it is observed, moves from one place to another without traversing the intervening space, can be in two places at once, and can influence other particles at a distance.

As it turned out, Jon and I stayed in contact and had lunch together periodically. He'd just moved back to town when I saw him at the restaurant. A couple months later, after he'd talked with mutual friends from our pasts, and then seeing my name in the Barstow College schedule as a psychology instructor, he finally came to believe what I told him was true.

We were having lunch one day and he asked how I did it. "I've tried a hundred times to clean up," he said, "but I can never do it."

I said, "Jon, did you know that an electron can move from one place to another without having traversed the intervening space?"

He just looked at me and shook his head. He wasn't impressed a bit. "So what! Is this the way educated people answer simple fucking questions?"

I laughed, then told him that I recovered in a residential substance abuse education program when I was in prison. Without going through the

167

entire process that I explained to Jon, I'll just say that when I left prison, I was certain that I wasn't going to drink or use anymore. I then explained to Jon that between the time I entered the program and my release from prison, I had recovered. I don't recall at what point this happened. In fact, I remember very little of that intervening space of time - similar to the intervening space that the electron traveled through that I mentioned earlier. I explained to Jon that I could not have done it on my own.

The vagabond that he is, Jon didn't stay in town very much longer. We both grew up here, so we kept in touch. I would go for long periods of time, sometimes years, before I'd hear from him again. He always had a reason for his reticence: "I went back to prison for a while," or "I got involved with a woman," or "I was on the lam." He had been doing drugs for forty years or more. Most people, including me, don't believe that he'll ever be free of drugs.

A few years later I got off work at six o'clock in the evening, went home and sifted through my mail, listened to my phone messages, then went to a restaurant for dinner. As I was waiting in line to pay my bill, the man in front of me turned around to leave and we made eye contact. "Wow, is that really you?" We had not seen each other in years. He said, "I've been clean and sober for two years, John."

I looked at him quizzically and said, "yeah, right!" Jon was *non compos mentis*. He was an ignominious liar and a con and had been for most of his life. Some people are just hopeless. When Roland H. called Carl Jung and wanted to be treated again for his alcoholism, Jung told him that his situation was hopeless. The only hope, Jung told him, was if he were the subject of a spiritual experience.

Jon smirked and said, "John, did you know that a manifestation of one quantum object, caused by our observation, simultaneously influences its twin object - no matter how far apart they are?"

"Oh, so now you're clean and sober and you're a quantum physicist? Do you have any proof?" Ironically, I had to meet someone in a bar that day, so I invited Jon to come along. We made small talk and asked about mutual friends, etc., then I asked if he wanted a drink. He said,

"No, John! I told you. I am clean and sober."

I smiled and told him I was just kidding. Then I asked him how he did it. He told me that even though he and I haven't been associating with each other for the last several years, that doesn't mean I wasn't still influencing him from-a-distance. Denny (2004) explains that "proponents of Era III medicine focus upon the nonlocal, action at-a-distance qualities of quantum particles as providing a rationale with which to support the theory that healing can occur between individuals at-a-distance." Jon then said, "John, you and I can be thought of as twin quantum objects - cut from the same mold, you might say - John and Jon. And it doesn't matter where I've been. You have definitely been influencing me."

Then, again, I woke up. I laid there for a while thinking of Jon and hoping that he was okay. As I was getting out of bed, the telephone rang. Bad news: it was one of Jon's friends calling to inform me that Jon was killed in a car accident the previous night. After talking with my friend's friend, I also found out, to my utter amazement, that Jon had been clean and sober for two years. I was flabbergasted. What a success story!

Von Franz (1992) wrote that "what Jung calls synchronicity refers to an accidental but meaningful coming together of an outer and an inner event. He had observed that individuals chiefly experience such coincidence when an archetype is especially intensively constellated in their unconscious" (p. 186). Was my dream a caveat? I had been feeling squirrelly lately, entertaining thoughts of hedone - like an orgy with the lovely Aphrodite and the blissful Morpheus. The street-like rebellious *puer* within had been rearing his flighty head recently. Was I not dreaming about Jon being clean and sober for two years? So which is it? Synchronicity, or Jon influencing me at-a-distance? Perhaps it's both. Maybe it's some kind of paradoxical wish fulfillment, or maybe the dream was having me - rather than the other way around.

Deutsch (September, 2001) shares that "even after someone dies, other copies of him might remain alive somewhere in the multiverse"(p.41); therefore, maybe we can continue to influence each other in the world of dreams whether we are dead or alive.

Conclusion

Whereas John and Jon are real people, none of the above events really happened. One statement in particular, however, is true: I have not seen Jon in more than 35 years. Whether there can be anything said positivistically concerning the quantum phenomenology of the above myth, I couldn't say. We, together with theoretical physicists, are aware that a quantum particle doesn't exist until it is observed, moves from one place to another without traversing the intervening space, can be in two places at once, and can influence other particles at a distance.

Chapter Seventeen References

Denny, Mike. (2004). "Walking the quantum talk." *Institute of Noetic Sciences Review*.

Folger, Tim. (2001, September). "Quantum Shmantum." *Discover*, 37-43.

Goswami, Amit. (1995). *The self-aware universe: How consciousness creates the material world*. New York: G.P. Putnam's Sons.

Von Franz, Marie-Louise. (1988). *Psyche and matter*. Boston, Massachusetts: Shambhala Publications, Inc.

CHAPTER EIGHTEEN

A Spiritual Quest

(Published in the Fall 2005 Issue of New Perspectives Magazine)

The past offers a profound resource to prove that culture, as much as individuals, moves through predictable stages of development that mirror the course of natural evolution. Drug addiction and criminality also go through a predictable developmental process. Criminalized male addicts (CMA) typically evolve, starting from the innocence of habilitated preteens, to the experimentation typical of adolescence, to the puerile behavior of adulthood, and finally into the criminal activity consistent with contemporary tricksters. An example of a modern day trickster is Frank Abagnale Jr., portrayed by Leonardo Dicaprio in *Catch Me If You Can*.

Is it worth considering what we can learn about CMAs that are different from the usual theoretical and statistical studies done on this population? Can an *understanding* of the archetypes being personified in CMAs help us to perceive them better? Will this perspective help us to learn why they don't respond well to treatment, and why their recidivism rates are so high? And what are the implications of them being on a spiritual quest?

Marie-Louise von Franz[1], a Jungian psychoanalyst and a protégé of Carl Jung, points out in *The Problem of the Puer Aeternus*: that "the man who is identified with the archetype of the *puer aeternus* remains too long in adolescent psychology; that is, all those characteristics that are normal in a youth of seventeen or eighteen are continued into later life."

In 1988, when I arrived on the prison yard, I saw a huge day-care center before me. Inmates were playing soccer, basketball, and throwing frisbees. They were working out on the weight pile, and playing cards on picnic tables. The tennis and handball courts were occupied, and others were cheering their favorite team while watching a softball game. In that *puer* country club, our clothes and linen were cleaned for us every week. They provided our meals. Every three months we could have money and material things (a package) sent to us from the outside. If we were married, we could even spend the weekend with our wives to relieve ourselves sexually.

Out of the 2.03 million inmates in this country today, according to Kipnis[2], drug offenders represent 60% of federal prisoners and over one-third of state and county prisoners. That doesn't include all the inmates who are incarcerated for crimes committed while under the influence, or the ones who were committing crimes for money to finance their chemical indulgences.

The archetypal development from *puer* to trickster coincides with addictive and criminal development. Before continuing, we must be kept reminded that development doesn't happen in strict conformity to predescribed phases - all addicts and criminals may not fit into this developmental process. There are those who get involved with criminal activity and never do drugs, and there are those who get involved with criminal activity prior to getting involved with drugs, and there are others who through grief, trauma, and a host of other disturbances pick up a dependency on substances later in life, and never participate in criminal activity. However, the process I am describing is the most common.

After the young adult has sewn his wild oats, he is traditionally expected to be developing into a responsible adult who either continues his education, embarks on a career, and/or gets married and starts a family. This doesn't usually happen with those who drink and use drugs. Instead, he continues behaving as though he were an adolescent. Fun takes priority. The *Fun Phase* correlates to the Peter Pan mentality of the *puer aeternus*.

Once this lifestyle is entrenched, the fun phase begins to get cluttered with periodic repercussions. Despite such inconveniences as having been kicked out of high school or college, being asked to leave home, getting fired from jobs, picking up a DUI or a possession charge, the flighty *puer* will continue going through girlfriends and jobs. This is the *Between Fun and Addiction Phase*.

172

By the time this phase is over, the high-flying *puer* has started his downward spiral. His legal problems inevitably increase. Often it's prison right away. Once criminalization and full-on psychological (sometimes physical) addiction sets in, the *jointster* (criminalized drug addict as trickster) has emerged.

Some authors suggest that the need to alter consciousness is innate - activities such as skydiving and water skiing, and other sports that increase adrenaline and incite endorphin activity, are consciousness-altering activities. Perhaps the internal needs to release inhibitions, be devious, act crazy, fight, gamble, have recreational sex, lie, cheat, and steal is also an innate need to alter consciousness, and serves as the impetus to personify the *puer* and trickster archetypes.

Andrew Weil[3], long before he became the guru he is thought of today, stated that "the ubiquity of drug use is so striking that it must represent a basic human appetite."

Christina Grof[4] (1993) is one who considers addiction as a path to wholeness:

> As far back into my childhood as I can remember, I was searching for something I could not name. Whatever I was looking for would help me to feel all right, at home, as though I belonged. If I could find it, I would no longer be lonely. I would be happy, fulfilled, and at peace with myself, my life, and the world. I would feel free, unfettered, expansive, and joyful.

Whereas Grof was searching for wholeness through alcoholism, perhaps criminalized drug addicts, with all of their puerile and trickster ways, are also on a spiritual search for wholeness.

Viewing *jointsters* through the archetypes and the spiritual quest, can give us an *understanding* that frees us from judgment, and allows us to see them as a breed of humanity different from ourselves. Perhaps some people are destined to live by organizing principles that we are unaware of. Perhaps there is far more than we would like to admit that we simply don't know. Perhaps many of our present theories are wrong.

Chapter Eighteen References

1. Von Franz, M. L. (2000). *The problem of the puer aeternus*. Toronto: Inner City Books, p. 7.

2. Kipnis, A. (1999). *Angry young men*. San Francisco: Jossey-Bass, p. 121.

3. Weil. A. (1972). *The natural mind*. Boston: Houghton Miflin Company, p. 17.

4. Grof, C. (1993). *The thirst for wholeness*. San Francisco: Harper, p. 9.

CHAPTER NINETEEN

Gridlock'd

After a synopsis of the movie *Gridlock'd*, and the characteristically authentic portrayals of Spoon and Stretch, I begin an analogue between the movie, my thoughts, and various writers to demonstrate a coalition between them. Among the writers that have written about the marginalized, Gloria Anzaldua offers her experience with rebellion to complement the rebellion that the two main characters in the movie display, at the same time adding more familiarity with the characters' predicament. Their predicament (hitting a bottom) leads my discussion into the recovery process using a brief alchemical analogy, and input from Jung. Spoon and Stretch (with help from Victor Turner) gives their rendition of play and ritual. Jung and Turner then offer words concerning the unconscious and the liminal that explain the trickster intelligence of these *Gridlock'd* addicts.

Synopsis
Gridlock'd, a realistic black comedy, revolves around three junkies. When the black woman of the trio overdoses, the salt and pepper duo, Spoon and Stretch, literally carries her to the emergency room where she remains in a coma during the rest of the movie. However, flashbacks offer us glimpses of the trio's relationship. This mismatched pair of societal misfits strives to seek help in kicking their heroin[1] habit in government-sponsored programs, only to find themselves depressingly being given the run-around from agency to agency. During their fruitless efforts toward rehabilitation, with cops hunting them and gangsters shooting at them, they are kept in a miasma of helplessness and demoralization. They finally wind up in the hospital - Stretch with a

---

[1] 1898, borrowed from German *Heroin*, a former trademark for this drug, registered in the 1890's by Friedrich Bayer and Company in Germany as a substitute for morphine. There is no evidence so far to indicate, as has been suggested, that the drug's name derives from Greek *heros* Hero, supposedly because of the euphoric feeling which the drug produces.

gunshot wound, and Spoon with knife wounds inflicted by Stretch with Spoons permission, in an attempt to get into the hospital where they could be out of harms way. The End

Discussion

Addicts, along with alcoholics (which are also addicts), ethnic minorities, prostitutes, homosexuals, ex-cons - just to name a few, are among the marginalized that populate many societies, especially our own. The esoteric nature of most of these groups tends to be subversive toward the dominant culture. Mexican lesbian Gloria Anzaldua (1999) believes that;

> ..a rebel dwells in her that she calls the Shadow-Beast. It is a part of me that refuses to take orders from outside authorities. It refuses to take orders from my conscious will, it threatens the sovereignty of my rulership. It is that part of me that hates constraints of any kind, even those self-imposed. At the least hint of limitations on my time or space by others, it kicks out with both feet. Bolts. (p. 38).

How well our two heroin addicts, Spoon and Stretch, demonstrate this repeatedly in the film. They rebel at the very drug they are addicted to because it had put their lady friend in a coma, which is what trigger their decision to kick the habit. They rebel with their acerbic remarks at the police, hospital staff, welfare workers, bureaucrats, and public transportation employees. They rebel and vituperate as they are shuffled around in a maze of bureaucracy - *Gridlock'd.* However, they are obviously intent on cleaning up.

Once immersed in the recovery process, one has become, in a way, reborn. However, this rebirth is a developmental process. This progression is from abstinence (learning how to stop using) to recovery (learning how to cope with life without substances) to comfortable living (learning how to live comfortably while abstinent) to productive living (learning how to build a meaningful clean and sober lifestyle). As in the art of alchemy, transformation requires a combination of elements. "Alchemy," says Gilchrist (1991) "is a discipline involving physical, psychological and spiritual work, and if any one of these elements is taken out of context and said to represent the alchemical tradition then the wholeness and true quality of alchemy is lost." (p. 1). This transformation is analogous to Jung's description of rebirth. Jung (1959) uses the Latin term *renovatio,* meaning renewal or renovation. "Rebirth," Jung writes;

> ..may be a renewal without any change of being, inasmuch as the personality which is renewed is not changed in its essential nature, but only its functions, or parts of the personality, are subjected to healing, strengthening, or improvement. Thus even bodily ills may be healed through rebirth ceremonies. (C.W. 9/1, par. 203).

I believe I was reborn in the state prison system where I was a resident in a substance-abuse education program. Between daily classes in the T.V. room of our dorm, a series of video tapes, books, pamphlets and group activity, I have since realized that I was, without knowing it at the time, going through a process of rebirth.

Since recovery is twofold - an obsession of the mind, coupled with a compulsion of the body, rebirth ceremonies are often integrated into the developmental process of recovery by celebrating various lengths of being clean and sber. Every year on May 7, for many years, I attended a rebirth ceremony where my cohorts awarded me with a cake and a coin that have my number of years of clean time inscribed on it. Unfortunately, *Gridlock'd* ends with us, the viewers, placing them either back into their netherworld of addiction, or actually succeeding in their quest for treatment. I prefer to believe they found recovery, but statistics suggest that they probably gave up and returned to active drug use.

Before either of them became drug addicts, we can assume that the development of their personalities during childhood was typical - whatever typical is. Then the substance monster arrived. As their dependence developed, so did a persona. They became different people than what they would have been had they not become immersed in the drug culture. Jung (1959) agrees that;

> The persona is that which in reality one is not, but which

177

oneself as well as others think one is. In any case the temptation to be what one seems to be is great, because the persona is usually rewarded in cash. (C.W. 9/I, par 221).

With Spoon and Stretch it was drugs rather than cash. The drugs turned both of them into a couple of tricksters. The trickster, Sharp (1991) reminds us, is "psychologically, descriptive of unconscious shadow tendencies of an ambivalent, mercurial nature." (p. 139). More on the trickster archetype later.

Chemical dependency in the lives of many can be thought of as unconscious shadow tendencies of an ambivalent, mercurial nature. Most people start imbibing at a young age, before the notion of "consequences" has had a chance to mature in their minds. Even after they do mature, after many years of reckless behavior involving jails and institutions, loss of families and jobs, wrecked cars, forsaken friendships, lying, stealing, and manipulating, the behavior continues with them being oblivious to the damage they have done to themselves and others - especially others. Jung agrees when he wrote that;

> It is often tragic to see how blatantly a man bungles his own life and the lives of others yet remains totally incapable of seeing how much the whole tragedy originates in himself, and how he continually feeds it and keeps it going. Not consciously, of course - for consciously he is engaged in bewailing and cursing a faithless world that recedes further and further into the distance. (C.W. 9/II, par. 18).

I can attest to what Jung is referring to. It was not until I was reborn that I was able to grow from an external locus of control to an internal locus of control. The fault, despite what or where it was, was not mine, or so I thought. The word "accountability" was not in my vocabulary. We see Spoon and Stretch in a whirlwind of bad luck. They think that God, fate, and/or the entire world are out to get them. One of the social workers they encounter recognizes their external locus of control and lets them have it with some of his own rebellion:

178

Am I supposed to change the rules because you're setting over there *screaming* at me? Take a look at ya - you fuckin walk in here after, what?, five, ten years, and because *this* is the day that you decide to kick! THE WHOLE [at this point the social worker's voice is screaming back at them] FUCKING WORLD IS SUPPOSED TO STOP? IS THAT IT? We all have been waiting for the day that you come through that door to tell us that YOU NO LONGER WANT TO BE A FUCKING DOPE FIEND. RIGHT? Get the fuck away from my desk.

Heroin addicts like Spoon and Stretch are unconscious of the wreckage they cause, especially when they are so continuously preoccupied with their endless search for the bag and their subsequent ritual with their needles and spoons. The shape of early spoons, by the way, can be found in the origin of their name. "Spoon" is from the Anglo-Saxon *spon*, meaning "chip," which gives us a curious anomaly: back in the fifties and early sixties, we used to refer to someone who was *not* addicted to, but used heroin, as one who just chips - a chippy.

Concerning the boys' ritual with needles and spoons, in "Body, Brain, and Culture," Turner (1987/88) explains that the ergotropic system affects behavior in the direction of arousal, heightened activity, and emotional responsiveness. The trophotropic system makes for inactivity, drowsiness, sleep, and trance-like states. (p. 9). Turner asks "where does 'play' play a part in this model? One seldom sees much mention of play in connection with brain neurophysiology. Yet play is a kind of dialectical dancing partner of ritual and ethologists give play behavior equal weight with ritualization." (p.12).

Our *Gridlock'd* junkies exhibit both ritualization and play behaviors. First I'll address play. Addicts, for the most part, are emotional retards. Again I quote Nakken:

> *Adolescents usually live for the moment. Practicing addicts are also living for the present moment, using emotional logic. Emotionally, addicts act like adolescents and are often described as adolescent in behavior and attitude. After all, a lot*

179

of issues addicts struggle with are the same issues that face adolescents. The difference is that addicts stay trapped in an adolescent stage as long as their addiction is in progress. (p. 16).

When Spoon and Stretch are talking to their buddies, having sex with their women, copping drugs, practicing their profession as musicians at gigs - they are playing. Their lives are spent relentlessly chasing the bag so they can continue to play.

Now I'll address ritual, which they combine with play. Here is how: they make a score; they go to their apartment (or the closest place); they break out their works (spoon, rig[2], tie, etc.); they pour the junk into the spoon (sometimes a bottle cap, which Spoon uses instead of a spoon); they draw water into the syringe and squirt it into the spoon; they use a lighter to heat the bottom of the spoon to dissolve the junk; they drop a small piece of cotton into the liquid; they put the eye of the needle into the cotton and draw the liquid into the syringe until the cotton is dry; they push the air out of the syringe with the plunger; they tie off their arm (sometimes using a belt if nothing else is available); they find a vein and . . ., zippity, do da, they are in a halcyon of chemical bliss for a couple hours, then they're off and running again.

Surprisingly, this ritual is a large part of the submersion into intravenous drug use. If heroin is not available, which inevitably happens periodically, most any substitute drug will do. We witness these two fabulists perform their *fabula tantum* as they joke around and banter - similar to how "normal" people behave when sitting around a coffee table imbibing in their less radical addictions.

Rituals such as these are so ingrained that they perform them unconsciously. But how can they be unconscious if those who are performing them are awake and alert? Jung (1969) explains:

> Between "I do this" and "I am conscious of doing this"
> there is a world of difference, amounting sometimes to

---

[2] Syringe' origin before 1398 as *syringa* - a catheter or a tube for irrigating wounds, etc.

outright contradiction. Consequently there is a consciousness in which unconsciousness predominates, as well as a consciousness in which self-consciousness predominates. This paradox becomes immediately intelligible when we realize that there is no conscious content which can with absolute certainty be said to be totally conscious, for that would necessitate an unimaginable totality of consciousness, and that in turn would presuppose an equally unimaginable wholeness and perfection of the human mind. So we come to the paradoxical conclusion that there is no conscious content which is not in some other respect unconscious. (C.W. 8, par. 385).

Two beat cops stop Spoon and Stretch coming out of an apartment building where a murder was just committed. As the officers put these two tricksters through the third degree, their blatant lying comes naturally - possibly unconscious. Hyde (1998) emphasizes that

The trickster myth derives creative intelligence from appetite. It begins with a being whose main concern is getting fed and it ends with the same being grown mentally swift, adept at creating and unmasking deceit, proficient at hiding his tracks and at seeing through the devices used by others to hide theirs. Trickster starts out hungry, but before long he is master of the kind of creative deception that, according to a long tradition, is a prerequisite of art. (p. 17).

A better example would be the distrait that most of us go through when we're driving down the freeway and pass the off ramp that we intended to get off on. We were conscious or we would not have been driving a motor vehicle, but we were unconscious because we have mildly dissociated.

The movie ends with our lugubrious duo - one shot in the arm and the other suffering from stab wounds, waiting to be treated in a sadly antagonistic emergency room. Their plight; however, could place them in an agonistic, liminal state of transition - recovery. Assuming that our

181

puerile, burnt-out junkies have truly started on the royal road to recovery, Turner (1966) would consider them "*liminal* entities, similar to neophytes in initiation or puberty rites, being represented as having nothing. They may be disguised as monsters, wear only a strip of clothing, or even go naked." Turner's continuing description sounds remarkably similar to people in recovery programs:

> Their behavior is normally passive or humble; they must obey their instructors implicitly, and accept arbitrary punishment without complaint. It is as though they are being reduced or ground down to a uniform condition to be fashioned anew and endowed with additional powers to enable them to cope with their new station in life. Among themselves, neophytes tend to develop an intense comradeship and egalitarianism. (p. 95).

Conclusion:

The marginalized have a friend in depth psychology. Though the *Gridlock'd* pair of junkies never find recovery on the screen, they did, however, in the sequel they performed in my mind. Gloria Anzaldua understands their rebellious nature by sharing with them the Shadow Beast that dwells within her. The recovery process they were so desperately trying to find escapes them. Gilchrist explained to them how addicts, like copper - do not want to be turned into gold. Carl Jung offers them a chance at being reborn but they choose to rip off a pair of dead drug dealers instead who were murdered. Jung even tried to explain to them that their radical behavior really isn't "they," but a persona. How convincing their persona is when even they believe it. Jung tried a third time to convince them that some of their behavior is unconscious, though they are wide awake and aware of what they are doing. Hyde and Sharp even explain to them how their personas have manifested as tricksters. Little do they know, when they start practicing a recovery program, they really will start turning into gold. Victor Turner tried putting their feelings at ease by explaining that their play is a kind of dialectical dancing partner of their rituals. In my mind these two addicts are sitting in a meeting somewhere telling others of their experience, strength and hope.

Chapter Nineteen References

Anzaldua, Gloria. (1987). *Borderlands: The new mestiza.* San Francisco: Aunt Lute Books.

Barnhart, Robert K. (1995). *The Barnhart concise dictionary of etymology: The origins of* American English words. New York: HarperCollins Publishers.

Gilchrist, Cherry. (1991). *The elements of alchemy.* Great Britain: Element Books Limited.

Hyde, Lewis. (1998). *Trickster makes this world.* New York: Farrar, Straus and Giroux.

Jung, Carl. (1960). *The structure and dynamics of the psyche.* New York: Pantheon Books.

Jung, Carl. (1959). *The archetypes and the collective unconscious.* New York: Pantheon Books.

Jung, Carl. (1959). *Aion.* Princeton, N.J.: Princeton University Press.

Nakken, Craig. (1988). *The addictive personality: Understanding compulsion in our lives.* San Francisco: Harper and Row Publishers.

Sharp, Daryl. (1991). *C.G. Jung lexicon: A primer of terms & concepts.* Toronto, Canada: Inner City Books.

Simpson, D.P. (1959). *Cassell's Latin dictionary.* New York: Macmillan Publishing Company.

Turner, Victor. (1966). Liminality and communitas. In *The Ritual Process.* Ithaca, NY: Cornell University Press.

Turner, Victor. (1987/88). *Body, brain, culture. In The Anthropology of Performance.* New York: PAJ Publications.

CHAPTER TWENTY

My Emerging Hermes

In my contribution to the symposium on Hermes I will try to show that this many-hued and wily god did not by any means die with the decline of the classical era, but on the contrary has gone on living in strange guises through the centuries, even into recent times (C.W. 13, par 193.).

Hermes, in the guise of John Smethers, has been alive and well in recent times. Hillman (1979) says that;

> Jung sensed the inherent opposition between Christianism and the underworld and attempted to darken the figure of Christ with Hermes-Mercurius. He did not go as far as Hades, but he did place Hermes-Mercurius as archetype of the unconscious in opposition to Christ as archetype of the upperworld's consciousness (p.89).

When I entered the parlous terrain of junior high school, Christ coalesced archetypally with Hermes as the trickster.

Developmentally, Hermes was becoming manifest in my unconscious. My callow entrance into junior high was simultaneously my refractory entrance into a netherworld. Hermes the trickster - the reputed thief, did not rear his sticky fingers in my life until later. However, junior high school was when I started chronic alcohol consumption. This ignominious lifestyle, which later included drugs, continued until I was in my mid forties.

In fragment 38, Heraclitus says it well: "When he is drunk, thus having his soul moist, a man is led about by an immature boy, stumbling and not knowing where he is going." Whether he meant it or not, he describes the *puer aeternus.* It was after graduating from high school

184

that I began experimenting with drugs. Hillman (1979) tells us that;

> We need incantations to summon Hypnos or Hermes to help us drop off to sleep, a ritual of prayer, toothbrushing and teddy bear, of masturbation, food cramming, and the late show, of nightcap and sleeping pill. The basic bedtime story of our culture is that to sleep is to dream and to dream is to enter the House of the Lord of the Dead, where our complexes lie in wait. We do not go gentle into that good night (p 34.).

I ran the gamut in the University of the Lord of the Dead, specifically in Hades' school of sleeping pills and nightcaps; his school of fornication and masturbation, and his continual messaging of Hermes to keep these traditions alive.

I was tricky and at the same time laudable. I was *semper fidelis* - always faithful to my friends, but would steal for and from the Augean stables[3] of my then flagitious employers - the outlaws of the service station business (see my article Lube Bay Bandits) on my website www.JohnSmethes.com. Brown (1990) explains that;

> Modern scholars have felt obliged to brand the cult of Hermes the 'tricky' as immoral. On the other hand, Hermes' name is 'the tricky,' but his function is to promote human welfare, the function implied by the epithets 'giver of good' and 'giver of joy' (p. 22).

We see here a double nature that is characteristic of me during my years in the underworld. I was under the aegis of the opposing archetypes of Hermes and Christ. I was also under the aegis of the dual archetype of *puer* and *senex*, but for purposes of brevity, I will not expound on the latter, since there's plenty of that in other papers of this book. And of course I'm under the aegis of the trickster of Indian mythology as the wily coyote.

---

[3] Augeas, the mythical king of Elis, kept great stables that held 3,000 oxen and had not been cleaned for thirty years - until Hercules was assigned the job. Hercules accomplished this task by causing two rivers to run through the stables.

Hillman (1979) reminds us of two kinds of consciousness: "for Hermetic consciousness, there is no upperworld versus underworld problem. Hermes inhabits the borderlines" (p. 180). I have never fully entered one world. I also sat on the borderline, but society insisted on keeping me marginalized and criminalized - *a hoc opus* - this was the difficulty. My friends and family have always trusted me, for I was, and still am, an honorable and trustworthy person, so Christ was present archetypally in my upperworld consciousness. Nevertheless, I straddled a scabrous line with - *blandae mendacia linguae*–lies of a smooth tongue, accompanied with a *modus operandi* of Hermetic stealing, Dionysian drinking, and Aresenian fighting. The Christian ethic and the Hermetic lifestyle make strange bedfellows. Hopefully, there is a Valhalla[4] for souls like mine. If not, *mea culpa*.

---

[4] In Norse mythology, the souls of warriors who died nobly in battle were brought to a magnificent palace, where they spent their days fighting for diversion, immune from lasting injury, quaffing freely-flowing mead. In Old Norse, the word for this warrior heaven is "Valholl" (literally, "hall of the slain"); in German, it is "Walhalla." (word@MERRIAM-WEBSTER.COM).

CHAPTER TWENTY ONE

Interviews With Probation Officers

Introduction

Having been an inveterate alcoholic and drug addict for more than thirty years, I was in continual contact with the supposedly rectitudinous police officers, jail and prison guards, and parole and probation officers (PO's). There was scarcely a time during those years that I was not either incarcerated, on parole or probation, pending court, or paying fines or restitution. During those years I developed an ignominious attitude (hate really) toward the people in those professions. I had the "us and them" attitude. Many people see the following as dichotomous: inmates and guards, PO's and their case loads, and cops and those who are involved in criminal activity. We often see this opposition in various forms of media, especially on TV, the news, and in motion pictures.

As explained in previous papers in this book, I have investigated the psychology of the *puer aeternus*, and the *senex*. Since I consider myself, and many others like me, a characteristic *puer*, I naturally came to the conclusion that my adversaries are characteristically *senex*. The *senex* archetype, says Hillman, (1970) promulgates law and order. (p. 149). Hillman (1989) describes personifications of the *senex* as "in the holy or old wise man, the powerful father or grandfather, the great king, ruler, judge, ogre, counselor, elder, priest, hermit, outcast and cripple" (p. 208). I've added prison guards, PO's and cops to the list.

During my research I've found that *us* and *them* are not really so different. Hillman (1970) explains "that the *senex* is a *complicatio* of the *puer*, infolded into *puer* structure, so that *puer* events are complicated by a *senex* background." (p. 146). Explaining that the *senex* has a double nature, Hillman continues by saying "one characteristic is never safe from inversion into its opposite." (p. 148).

Research Question

My research took me to those former adversaries to discover the ethos of their respective working environments. I also interviewed police officers and correctional officers, but the research in this paper is restricted to probation officers. Are we really so different? Are we the same? Are we both? How many outlaws of the old west later turned into lawmen? How many cops or entire police departments *are* Augean stables[5], bringing opprobrium and embarrassment on their profession?

Assumptions

I attended a meeting of the *Claremont Forum* where four panelists were giving talks about prison, each coming from their personal or professional backgrounds. The first panelist was Gil Contreras, a former Los Angeles police officer - rampart division, who was a journalist at the time. Gil's *mea culpa* promulgated a *modus operandi* that generally does not get talked about - especially in public and on videotape. Having been a law enforcement officer, his credentials are impressive, which include being a qualified gang and narcotics expert. Gil talked about cop culture - a culture fraught with dishonesty, corruption and shadow. He described cop culture as being comparable to gang culture.

During my addiction I believed that I did not hurt anybody except myself. I thought my crimes were victimless - I *was* the victim, or so I thought. My question was, what kind of imperious system locks people up for crimes against themselves? Prior to recovery, I was a bartender in a biker bar. I won't elaborate on that here since I covered it in a previous paper in this book.

Method

Since I am familiar with the probation department in Barstow, I contacted the department head, Mr. K, a white middle-aged man. Having previously worked as a field officer, and presently as a court liaison and investigator, he also does the initial interviews with prospective probationers. I explained that what I was asking of him, was not a traditional interview - that I would ask just one question and

---

[5] Augean stable most often appears in the phrase "clean the Augean stable," which usually means "clear away corruption." Derives from Augeas, the mythical king of Elis.

he would talk for twenty minutes in response to that question. The question, I said, is in the title of the study: *The Probation/Parole Ethos as Described by Probation/Parole Officers: A Phenomenological Stud.* He signed an informed consent form, and I turned on my tape recorder. Afterward he introduced me to two other probation officers, and I later repeated the same process with them. As they presented their various perspectives, I listened, nodded my head, smiled when appropriate, and gave them the respect of an honest interest in what they were saying.

The theoretical method I was using is called phenomenological. The purpose of phenomenological interviewing, according to Marshall and Rossman, (1999) "is to describe the meaning of a concept or phenomenon that several individuals share." (p. 112). Prior to interviewing, I wrote a description of my experiences and bracketed them from those of the interviewees. This is referred to as *epoche.* The purpose of this is to gain clarity from my preconceptions. The next phase is called *phenomenological reduction*; here, I identified the essence of the phenomenon. I then clustered the data around *themes* that describe the experience. And the last stage, *structural synthesis*, involves the imaginative exploration of all possible meanings and divergent perspectives and culminates in a description of the essence of the phenomenon and its deep structure. (p. 113). Whereas each of Marshall and Grossman's phases were adhered to, the sequence might be out of order.

Data
My first interview with the above-mentioned officer of the *San Bernardino County Probation Department* started with him explaining the general backgrounds of the people who are on probation at any given time. He mentioned ethnicity and culture, family, criminal activity, and drug and alcohol involvement. One of the buzz words he was consistent in using was "behavior." He used it in relation to society's norms and how the probationers interact with their environment. Mr. K referred to himself and his colleagues as "we." He said that "we are sometimes working in the capacity of a cop and sometimes in the capacity of a social worker - the job being a combination of both." Often probation officers must require people to do things that they do not want to do. When they do not comply, then they are locked up. However, Mr. K appeared more interested in

helping people rather than locking them up. Having also mentioned the manipulative nature of many probationers, he admitted that locking up those types is best for everybody concerned. Otherwise, they will not learn to be accountable for their actions. Most of the rest of the interview consisted of small talk and cultural idiosyncrasies of various groups.

The second interview was with an approximately thirty-five year old white male named Mr. C: a juvenile probation officer. Mr. C first described his jurisdiction geographically and explained the relationship he has with his partner. He talked about the differences between juvenile and adult offenders and how it is much easier to scare juveniles into reforming their ways than it is adults. Mr. C was able to quote statistics concerning those who do and those who don't successfully terminate probation. He also made it clear how important the roles of the parents are before, during and after they come in contact with the probation department. *Project Focus*, the brainchild of the probation department in Barstow, hosts several programs that are often mandatory, especially for juvenile offenders. These programs address substance abuse, anger management, gang intervention, etc. Mr. C also explained the role that the *Youth Accountability Board* plays in the community, which is designed mainly for first offenders. The findings of this board usually get the kid off with community service or one of the programs mentioned above, and the offense that got him there is quashed, unless criminal behavior starts again. An ongoing requirement, said Mr. C, was the continual reports that have to be filled out by probation officers, which results in a long paper trail that documents the processes of the offenders from beginning to end. He also concurred that substance problems are an ever-present deterrent to the successful termination of probation. This interview was fraught with the job's legal aspects, technical requirements, statistics, and program management concerning *Project Focus* and other programs; however, he seemed genuinely concerned for his probationers with a strong desire to see them succeed. Mr. C also mentioned, several times, the importance of background - family dynamics, school and criminal history, etc. He also talked about facets of the field that entails taking kids into custody, handcuffing, carrying a gun, and sometimes violent encounters. Mr. C and his partner are associated with many community agencies such as the *School Attendance Review Board, Youth*

Accountability Board, *Project Focus*, and the local high schools - among others. An aspect of the job as a field officer, includes a certain amount of danger, he said. Though he did not elaborate extensively on this, he did make it clear that field officers need to be in good physical condition and be ready to use a firearm when necessary; however, the carrying of firearms is optional. During the concluding minutes of the interview he explained the requirements for the job and how much he enjoys working with juveniles(as opposed to adults.

The concluding interview was with a middle age black woman named Miss S. She identified herself as an adult investigating officer of the *San Bernardino County Probation Department.* She spent most of the time talking about various reports, such as "pre-sentence reports, the 1203.3's and 1203.4's." Those numbers reflect two different types of dismissals. She elaborated extensively on the court process. She also focused on probation violation and its implications. Background information was also pertinent to the various reports required of her. She mentioned travel permits as a requirement before a probationer can leave the state, and what can happen to them if they fail to get one. Miss S is active with *Project Focus*, which hosts programs such as *Positive Alternatives* (a women's group), *Tools for Tomorrow* (adult batterers program), *Freedom from Substance Abuse for Youth*, *Choices* (a youth group for teens between 14 & 18) among others. Not all of those programs are currently available She talked about how the job is two-faceted - part law enforcement and part social work. She feels that currently the pendulum is swinging more on the punishment side, and because of that she feels the department is lacking in credibility. Miss S spent much of the remaining time talking about her feelings about the job - the positive and negative aspects of it, the integrity of the department, and ended by stating that she loves her work, regardless of the pitfalls.

Limitations

This research project did not go well. It is laden with problems from the start. First of all, I pressed *Play* instead of *Record* with three interviews; therefore, I ended up with none. I had to go back and do it again, which took me a month. I interviewed two of the same people again, which probably skewed my findings because after the first interview I told them the reason for my research. Another one I recorded was not legible because an air conditioner was running in the background, so after that I used a boom box rather than the little hand-held type of recorder. The probation department in Barstow is small: therefore their staff is small. Ideally, interviews with just adult field officers would have been more suitable to my reasons for interviewing probation officers. I also believe I could've phrased the research question better. Though I provided a definition to the word *ethos* for all of them before the first interview, we relied on their memory for the second interview. For the sake of brevity, I will not list any more limitations. I could, however, write an entire paper about the limitations of this study. By the time I was finished with the course work for my Ph.D., I'd gotten better at interviewing research subjects, which is undoubtedly the reason for these research projects prior to the research required for the dissertation.

Themes

All three of my interviewees discussed the probationers' backgrounds: family, culture, criminal activity, education, etc. Drugs and alcohol were also mentioned by all of them, especially concerning urinalysis and violation of probation; however, two of them talked about it only in reference to the various reports they had to make. Another obvious congruence was their relative discussion of the court system and the decisions that judges make. One of the most intriguing themes between them was how they expressed their methods of forcing probationers to change, which ultimately results in either the desired change or jail time. To quote one of them: "We tell people what *we think* is the best thing for them." All of them concurred that the job was a combination of being a cop and a social worker. Understandably, all of them commented on the effectiveness of *Project Focus*. Unfortunately *Project Focus* is no longer available.

Appendix

As I stated earlier, this study is lacking in many areas. Each PO spoke from their specific roles as probation officers. One is a department head, one is a juvenile PO, and one is an investigator. At first I thought that diversity was a plus. With an air of circumspection, one of them complained a lot about the politics of the department, which took up half the interview, but this did not surface during the other two interviews. One of the others spent much of the time talking about the ethnicity of his family members, using them as a comparison to probationers. The other one focused almost entirely on legal aspects. All this tells me that I probably did not ask the right question in the first place. Or, I did not phrase the question correctly.

During the many years I spent on probation and parole, I prejudged PO's as acerbic vermin. I formed very similar opinions about cops and guards too. What kind of a human being, I wondered, could enjoy a job that makes the lives of other people miserable? Of course, this was before I learned about internal and external loci of control. The reason I mention this, is that I may have brought some of this attitude with me into my clean and sober life - into my supposedly internal locus of control. Is it possible, therefore, that I wanted to interview PO's to substantiate my image of them? My opinion of cops was certainly reinforced when Gil Contreras spoke about cop culture. My attitude was: I am better than them because my humanity was not enhanced at the cost of human misery.

I am unable to determine for sure whether the probation officers were truly sincere. However, what I heard was sanguine - caring and compassionate people who are working to help people change and live productive lives.

Addendum
One of the other two probation officers that I interviewed who is not a part of this study, did reinforce my previous image of probation and parole officers. I suspect that it was him and his partner that Miss S was speaking of when she commented that "the department's pendulum is currently swinging toward the cop side of the job."

Chapter Twenty One References

Hillman, J. (1970). "On senex consciousness." *Spring: An Annual of Archetypal Psychology and Jungian Thought.*

Hillman, James. (1989). *A blue fire.* New York: Harper and Row Publishers.

Jung, C.G. (1967). Alchemical Studies. Princeton, N.J.: Princeton University Press.

Marshall, Catherine & Rossman, Gretchen B. (1999). *Designing qualitative research.* Sage Publications: Thousand Oaks, CA.

To contact the author:

John E. Smethers, Ph.D.
904 S. Second Ave,
Barstow, CA 92311
USA

Tel: 760-256-8266

www.JohnSmethers.com
email: gwakwa@gmail.com

www.ingramcontent.com/pod-product-compliance
Lightning Source LLC
Chambersburg PA
CBHW072231270326
41930CB00010B/2078